HIGH PERFORMANCE HABITS

Achieve Extraordinary Results Transforming Your Life Through Powerful Habits And Becoming An Extraordinary Person

Table of Contents

Introduction 3
HABITS FOR HEALTH AND PHYSICAL WELL-BEING 16
How to become a successful person 18
How to Have a Good Performance Habit 23
Creating a high performance team 27
The Characteristics of People Who Evolve Faster Than Others 29
Habits That Can Help You Achieve Long-Term Success and Resonant Well-Being No Matter Your Career, Age, Strengths, or Personality 84
Practical High-performance habits that will make you successful 93
How to Get Ahead When You Are At Your Limit and Without Strength 102
Improve productivity by recognizing your personal values and motivations 116
To Become A High Performer, You Must Seek Clarity, Generate Energy, Raise Necessity, Increase Productivity, Develop Influence, and Demonstrate Courage 147

Introduction

Without doubt, there are only few people in the world who managed to maintain a high level of performance and personal satisfaction while still prolong their success for several decades. To maintain this longevity in success, there are some habits that you can put into practice.

One of the aspirations of the majority of people is the combination of both success and happiness. Having aspire for that greater heights, the question usually attached is, how can you be successful and have a feeling of satisfaction? In this book you could get the answers.

You will learn about the habits that you must adopt so that you can move from being an ordinary person into an extraordinary person. This book relates the habits adopted by extraordinary people to become what they are and how they achieve the feat. Through a vast exploration and extensive study of data obtained from the information gathered to analyze the successful and productive people in the community. You will be shown the habit that you must adopt and develop to create a very successful career.

Various methods are explained, seeking clarity, generating energy, raising the needs, increasing productivity, developing influences while demonstrating courage are a few habits that must be developed in reaching your goals. You will learn how to take up these habits, practice them and persevere, no matter how long it takes to achieve your aim. With a goal of feeling of satisfaction and end reward, how to make the sacrifice and persistency is encouraged. Following the steps discussed in this book promises a big difference in your life, you will become more effective and productive while having greater influence in your daily life, both at home and at work. Your level of productivity will increase you begin to have more influence and confidence to face all challenges, this will propel you towards achieving greater heights.

This book serve as an invitation to practice the habits that propels you to the top and make you maintain your level of success at the top within a short period of time, you begin to dominate the habits and it becomes part of your day to day life, you improve gradually till you find yourself at the top while enjoying success for a very long time.

The question is, why do some people or team enjoy success more than others while being able to maintain that level of success for a very long time?

What is that thing which they do spectacularly which others couldn't do?

Having a realistic goals and expectations

Setting a realistic goal and an expectation is a major character of Harry. Before he set a particular goal, he makes sure he studies the subject thoroughly. He read books, makes research, ask questions and seek advice from friends. He make sure he learns about his goal, he measures his goal, make sure it is reasonable and achievable.

Meanwhile, Fred does not do any findings or research before venturing into a new adventure. He is a person who always wants to start immediately, he does not want to waste time. To him, losing more than 40 pounds within two weeks seems a reasonable goal to him. He likes to chase a goal without asking questions if the goal is measurable, achievable, realistic or can be achieved within a time frame or not. He just dives into the river with both legs.

Allocation of time while setting up a new goal

Harry knows deep inside him that to achieve a certain goal, he has to take his time to get there, although he might have a tight schedule, he knows that to achieve his aim, he has to forfeit some activities. Harry knows that if he can't assign a time in achieving his goal, then it's unnecessary to start the goal.

Meanwhile, Fred also has a very tight schedule, but he only thinks he can find an extra time to achieve his goal. He always thinks that things will automatically be put in place without assigning some efforts.

Measuring progress and setting milestone

Harry knows that the success of setting up a goal its dependent on the measure of such goal. Goal must be measurable. Just as you know that measuring your weight alone is not enough to set a goal of weight reduction. You have to measure the percentage of your body fat to enable you to take the right measures for weight loss.

Based on the measure of this goal, a time frame can then be set to enable him to achieve his goal. Harry then structure a befitting program for himself to achieve the goal he has set, he either set a daily, weekly or monthly program to enable him to achieve his goal. This can also enable him to check his progress, he can check if he is on through right track of realizing his goal or not. If he doesn't achieve his aim within the stipulated time, he knows his strategy is not working, he has to try another.

Fred doesn't care about measuring his progress, he is the type that wants to lose up to 40 pounds but he has no idea on the rate of work out he should be doing daily, weekly or monthly. He only thinks he can lose the weight by looking at the mirror or listening to opinions of people around him. He thinks with this, he would just jump on the scale on day and find his weight reduced by 40 pounds.

Maintaining steady progress vs maintaining abrupt progress

Harry, while setting up his goal knows deep down that he has to start steadily, he has to learn few things and to test the water with a foot before jumping into the river. He makes sure that he starts by playing it safe and effective.

While planning to reduce few pounds, he begins by eating healthy food, phasing out unhealthy food. While at the training ground, Harry tries to get to his limit, he keeps on pushing on, he bid his time, making sure he learns how to carry out each exercise properly, then he gradually increases his challenges, making sure he exceeds his limits.

Fred, while setting up his goals, he knew he has never worked on it before, but he does not want to allocate time to the exercise, he only wants instant result. He only heard that a certain diet is effective at losing weight, without making proper research, he gets to it completely.

He visits the gym or training ground, jump to the activity if the day, he doesn't even learn the basics, neither did he warm up or learn how to carry out the exercise properly.

Having a Quick fix rather than a long-term strategy

Harry believes in a philosophy, that "Quick fix doesn't last." therefore, when he makes a decision on embarking on a goal, he makes sure that he chooses a strategy which is viable in the long run. He doesn't choose the quick fad diet; he chooses a diet with a routine that lasts forever.

Fred is the guy who just wants to reach his goal quickly and then forget about it and continue with his life. He wants fast results, he wants to get slim, but he doesn't want to sacrifice his diet, he believes in taking pills and steroids to lose weight. He just wants to get slim at a go.

Mentoring

Harry knows that he needs to consult an expert to guide him and help him accelerate his progress, that enables him to minimize mistakes along the way. He bids his time in consulting the right expert to guide him through the basics, he doesn't mind taking some coaching sessions to find out the best steps he can embrace to effectively achieve his goal. Harry does not mind hiring a dietician who guide him towards what's good for his body and what's not. He doesn't mind changing his feeding roster to achieve his goal.

Fred does not consult anyone, he felt he does not need anyone to tell him what to do and what not to do. He believed he has read a few magazines on fitness and diet. So, he believed he has a strategy that should work out for him. He sees no need for routine exercises, he only does the exercises he wishes to do on a daily basis. For Fred, to hire a dietician is a waste of time and money, he believes no one knows his body better than himself. Based on some columns and articles he read on a newspaper, he believes has developed his own diet.

Taking responsibility

Besides having a mentor or trainer, Harry knows the essence of social support in achieving his goals. He believes that the people around him plays a crucial part in the achievement of his goal. He therefore, move with friends of like minds, friends who will encourage him positively. He does not reveal his plan to people who are always thinking negatively, people who will discourage him.

Harry understands that it is important to be surrounded by positive thinkers. He sets up a pact with one of his friends to go to the nearby gym every evening, at least 4 times a week. He knows he will be motivated by his friend and checked if he fails in his promise.

As for Fred, he tells everyone the new goal he has set for them to be aware that he has new plans, he does not care whether he will be encouraged or discouraged. He does not keep his social circle in check, he does not look for a circle of people who eats healthy or keep exercise. He depends on his own intuition and he does not believe he needs anyone around to motivate him.

Do it for the right reasons

Harry's main aim of losing weight is because he wants to be healthier, fitter and happier while also be a source of inspiration to others. Due to this, Harry set his goals for the right reasons and when things go hard, he is persistent. Harry knows he does not need to be proud, walk haughty and show off his success. Rather, he works silently and understands the fact that rewards and fulfilling the rights of others comes after success, not bragging.

Fred always wants to impress everyone and feel above others. He loves to be considered better than others. More often than not, he often has to take a picture of himself at the beach, luxury hotels or at the gym. He dies this to find popularity and gather attention. His purpose doesn't stem from a deep desire to succeed rather, his purpose is to satisfy his ego. So, when things get harder, Fred could not muster courage he could not find the intrinsic motivation to keep on moving and never give up.

Few months later

Harry has already made some progress. He has weighed some pounds less while also developed a mass of muscle. The exercise plans he and his coach designed help him achieve his goals. He then increases his challenges and intensity of workout gradually. He then feels that his body becomes more and more stronger and he then becomes more flexible day by day.

After achieving his goal, he has little trouble in adjusting to his new diet, but now he feels better. Even occasionally, when he has to take fast food, since his body already has the required nutrients, it is then easy for him to adjust and stay on track.

Even when Harry wants to bend the rule, he allows himself a non-compliant meal once in a while, without the feeling of guilt, he knows he is on a good diet and breaking the rule taking one meal with which is less healthy food will change little.

For a few weeks, Harry was emotionally unstable, he felt depressed and he could not even do the things he used to do, not even his daily exercise. Fortunately, his friend, whom he had earlier made a pact with, was there to encourage him and motivate him. He lifted his spirit, he was able to take him around, even to the gym. This made him not to miss a single training and exercise at his toughest times.

Additionally, he has two colleagues and a sister who are obese. Seeing the wonders and body transformation done by Harry, they were inspired by the results, they also get motivated and start improving their lifestyle, with every one of them supporting one another and encouraging each other.

On the other side, Fred was faced with some difficulties, the diet plans he designed worked during the first week, but after that, he began to have some cravings, that is a sign that he lacks some essential nutrients. After a few days, his planned diet ended up at the McDonald's restaurant. He had the best meal in his lifetime.

Also, the exercises he planned for himself also worked well for few days until he injured his leg.

This incident prevents him from going to the gym for some days, negating all the progress he has made. After recovering from his leg injury, Fred failed to go to the gym for few more weeks because of the horror shock of his injury. It's obvious that no one was there to motivate him and encourage him to return to the gym.

During this period, Fred develops a rash on his body due to the use of steroid, he visited the doctor and drugs was prescribed to him to counterbalance the effects.

After a while, Fred starts to wonder if this type of lifestyle is meant for him. Besides, he could not point out any member of his family who is fit and healthy. Perhaps he starts to think his genes are problematic.

The illustrations given above are about loss of fat. However, this same principle is applicable to achieve any goal that we desire, we can follow the same process, whether we want to start a business, learn a sport, improve our health, or eager to achieve success in our relationship. To achieve our goals, we must make sure we follow the fundamental principles.

If you have a goal you wish to achieve but you feel you are not making the desired progress, make sure you follow the fundamental basics of success, ensure that your actions and strategy are similar to Harry's and not Fred's.

An important discovery in the field of psychology is that, about 95% of everything we think, do, feel and obtain are as a result of our habits. As we grow, we develop various types of responses either consciously or unconsciously, it is this response that leads us to react to situations in spontaneous and automatic way.

On the other hand, it could be said that all successful people have one thing in common, that is the "habits of succeeding," meanwhile, unsuccessful people do not have this trait. Every accomplished men and women who has good health status do say the right things, in the right way, and at the right time. They carry out these actions easily, automatically and in a coherent manner. This results in them getting more than what they want, sometimes they get 10 to 20 times more than what the people who have not get learned these habits yet.

In a more wider perspective, the ability to realize a dream, desires, expectations, hopes and goals in all areas of life is termed success.

Generally, 4 categories of goals are common to all

Physical well-being and health

Personal relationships: intimate, work, social and professional

Getting Financial independence

Job: getting a job, carrying out the job and getting paid for the job

Interestingly, all habits can be realized with lots of practice and repetition. All that is required is to look for the "good habits" that will be needed for achieving the goal you desire.

Classification of all the habits that could be used in realizing a goal;

Habit to be free financially

Habit for personal effectiveness

Habits of being hungry for success

Habits of self-valuation and growth in your professional career

Habits of the successful businessmen

Habits of getting along with people

Habits of successful sales

HABITS FOR HEALTH AND PHYSICAL WELL-BEING

The habits that enable you to develop great character and good leadership skills.

All habits cannot be treated extensively, therefore, in this chapter, some specific habits to be free financially will be discussed.

Assuming you are taking that bold step and you are starting with, let's say one million dollars, in the next (x) years, you will be achieving (....). Write down your objective, commit to the cause of achieving it, make a plan, and make sure you engage in an action that will bring you closer to your goal every single day. Every day, take your time and spend few minutes to read, visualize, review and evaluate your actions that will lead you towards achieving your goals.

Then make a well detailed analysis of your financial situation; your income, savings, expenses, debts, net worth etc. This analysis should be on a regular basis, weekly or monthly.

For your financial independence, you can open a current account, save about 10 - 20% of your income, make sure you do not spend this savings unnecessarily except if it is on investment and the growth of your business.

Protect yourself and your business with different insurance.

When you are in need, make sure you prioritize your needs and wants. Do not get carried away by the appearance and fashions. Do not buy just anything, except what you need. Be moderate in your expenses. Before investing your money in anything, make a research study before choosing among the different tools of investment.

In developing a new habit, there is a general rule, which is; be patient with yourself. Know that it is not possible to just change everything overnight. You are on the course of investing on yourself for a lifetime. So, firstly choose the first habit, develop it and integrate it before then going to the next one.

How to become a successful person

There is a universal step of climbing the ladder of success.

Believe in yourself, take action and do not accept any excuse that holds you back, and always keep focus; look for strategies to seek help in your projects, in case of hardships, do not be scared of making mistakes along the way and don't be afraid of taking unusual decisions.

Be courageous, be ambitious and when you see the signs of success, do not let yourself to be carried away by avarice, keep yourself in the midst of positive people and keep a cool head. That will assist you in progressing with your personal development and the development of your project.

Avoid the negative people, work harder, do not get distracted by the trolls and do not let anyone come in between you and your success. The question that arises is that, why are some people miserable while others are happy on their journey?

What exactly is that factor that motivates people to reach a higher level of success and what are the things they put into practice that help them improve? Burchard, the world's leading high performance coach carried out an extensive research, at the end of the research, he discovered that it is only six deliberate habits that gives you an edge, he said further, that anyone can carry out these habits deliberately and, when they do, they start to achieve extraordinary things, they achieve greater things in their lives, careers and relationships.

These habits can assist you in achieving long term success no matter your sex, age, personality, career or strength. To operate in a high level of success and enjoy a lasting success at the peak, there are certain things that must be done. You must seek clarity, develop influence, demonstrate courage, generate energy, raise necessity, and increase your level of productivity. In this book, you will learn about the art and science of how to practice and cultivate these proven habits.

Whether you want to improve certain part of your skills, be a good leader, want to increase productivity, or increase drastically, your sense of joy and confidence, the habits discussed in this book can assist you greatly and help you achieve it faster. Each of the six enlisted habits are practically explained with powerful thought provoking exercises, a cutting-edge science and real-world technique that you can implement.

The key habits that enables high performance

Search for clarity

More often than not, people with a very high performance do not wait till the eve of the new year before having a self-assessment and having to think about the type of change they want in their lives, rather, they seek clarity on a day to day basis, they are create a self-awareness of the changes in their lives. A simple way to deploy this, is to have more focus on these four things; skills, self-confidence, social and human service. Let's take for instance, how can you describe your ideal self? How do you want to interact socially? What are the skills you want to develop or improve? What are the services that you wish to render? These are the questions you should be frequently asking yourself.

Generating energy

Lots of people tend to lose energy while making a transit between different tasks, responsibilities or meetings. Meanwhile, people of extraordinary performance, when faced with such transition, try to dominate, they take some psychological break that releases them of some tension, doing this, they get relieved and renewed their approaches in facing each task. Every day they find a time to relax, and this boost their level of creativity.

Raise the need

It is important for you to know the psychological need of why you need to perform a function before you engage in a task. High performance people tend to have a deep sense of excellence and performing at their highest standards, this is associated with their identity. They have a passion to do things right, they dedicate their activity towards achieving the best possible result for their clients, teammates, or family. They always tend to do things perfectly.

Increase in productivity

This is a trait which is common to all high-performance geniuses like Bill Gates, Steve Jobs, Arianna Huffington and Oprah Winfrey. They know the importance of the end result. To be a productive person, you need to always be steps ahead and align yourself to achieve your goals while learning to manage anything that could cause distractions and avoid other forms of distractions.

Building a positive influence on others

Affecting people's lives, teaching them to reason, challenging them to grow and improve is essential. Also, having a positive impact in their lives, pushing them to their limit, awakening their flexibility and sensitivity is also crucial. Because, all those who are capable of making positive impact have a way of contributing towards the growth of others.

Demonstrate value

In the face of risk, fear of the unknown and difficulty. High performance people stand tall, they speak for themselves, keep their focus, and honor the struggle by adapting and learning to manage the situation. We can say that they "embrace" the difficult moments, instead of wailing and complaining or giving up, they identify their mission, keep their head cool, use it as a learning curve and sail the tide. They embrace the situation with purpose and make meaning out of it.

How to Have a Good Performance Habit

According to the popular saying "everything is in the mind," this statement turns out to be true while achieving a set goals, whether in business, education or sports. Being in a good state of the mind is a rule used for good performance, as this can enable you to focus, concentrate your energy and thoughts in achieving success. After getting this right, you can move further by polishing and perfecting a high-performance team.

Have a good performance under pressure

Sometimes, pressure and anxiety tend to reduce the performance of an individual or team drastically. The below steps can help you achieve a good performance, even while under an intense pressure.

1. Learn to control stress.

It is important to check and control the physical and psychological effects of stress. Having a little stress can lead you to feel the adrenaline negatively and this will definitely decompensate your body. Make sure you wash away stress, you can try having a light exercise, a good nap, seek social support, have some moments of fun or meditation or even engage in something that makes you feel relaxed.

2. Identify the things that you cannot control in any situation.

You should know that when your reaction towards every situation that faces you goes a long way towards your road to success. Don't waste your time on the things you cannot control, this will improve your mental stability and, in this way, it boost your level of productivity.

3. Replace negative thoughts with positive thoughts.

It's normal sometimes to think in a negative way about situations, changing your way of thinking may not come easy, but always remember this saying "take every risk and leave aside your fears," always be positive, persistent and patient. You also need to pay concentration on the things that matters to you.

4. Visualize success

One of the ways of achieving good performance in situations that comes with great challenges is by visualising the benefits, setting your eyes on the prize. Have you ever imagined facing a challenge and ending up being victorious?

5. Highlight your strengths

Your strength should be used to your advantage. For instance, let's assume that you are a sprinter, and you need to run a marathon race, one of your tactics will be to keep close to the rest, especially those who are ahead of you until you have the chance to increase your pace to win the race.

6. Stay motivated.

Keep yourself motivated, set goals for yourself, set small goals, bigger goals, short term goals and long term goals. Set goals for yourself, especially if you are working in a company that does have a good scheme for creating incentives.

7. Welcomes spirituality.

Embracing things that makes you comfortable, take for example, if you feel good while wearing a certain suit or you have a special pair of shoes that makes you feel confident, use them on occasion that are important to you, it can make you have a good performance. Although, superstition can arise when you have too many magical thoughts.

8. Face the flaws immediately.

On every activities that you engage in, you need to create a kind of emotional resistance by taking positive from the whole activities, learn your lesson after every failure. This will assist you in avoiding decadence of confidence.

9. After the failure, don't give up.

He who never fails has never tried something new, after failing, move on, repeat the same process without making the same mistake and return to the normal mood for the next performance.

Creating a high performance team

1. *Choose a first level team.*

Having a team that could be said to be first level includes having a team that works very well as a group of people while still having a healthy competition. Nevertheless, members must respect each other at all times.

2. *Establish team goals as well as individual goals.*

When you plan a certain goal for the whole team, make sure an incentive that entices everyone will be included, thus, you must ensure that every member is interested in the incentive.

3. *Let the whole group know how your attained success will be measured.*

These goals are based on the set standards, benchmarks and success evaluation.

4. *Always be honest about your strengths and weaknesses.*

A team can only function properly when they give sincere information and support for one another to cover all the bases and needs.

5. *Promoting the union in the team.*

Having a get together, going out for a few drinks or picnic once in a while is an effective medium to encourage members to support one another and strive to achieve the aim and goal of the team. With unity, both short-term and long-term goals can be realised.

6. *Eject a team member if the need arises.*

Perhaps in every disciple, there will be a Judaism, if any member of the group does not perform well, give an opportunity for correction. However, if that doesn't work, and the person is not fit into the group, tell such a person tactically that he belongs to somewhere else.

7. *Choose a leader or let the team choose the leader naturally.*

In addition, the leader should be a type of person who will be be willing to accept certain risks and be rewarded for their extra work.

8. *Let teamwork flow independently.*

In a team that is performing so well, there will always be some individual who are talented and compensate the team, sometimes their individual brilliance win it for the team. Let the teamwork compensate each other.

The Characteristics of People Who Evolve Faster Than Others

Lots of studies in psychology shows the importance of "attitude" adopted by every individual in their personal success and professional career. Attitude towards the day to day activities is crucial to the performance of every individual and this is a determinant of success. Successful people shows the right attitude towards every step they take.

Here are the 9 attitudes that allow some people to climb to the top leaving others behind:

1 - *They are humble, not arrogant*

A major traits of arrogance is that, it makes the arrogant one feels as if he knows it all, they think they have mastered everything. The one who is humble do believe that he still has lots of things to learn, he always wants to learn and improve, he never stops learning. People who are humble share their success with people rather than hoarding it, they know success is more often a product of cooperation, because of this, they always want to engage with people.

2 - *They seek to serve people before they are being served*

Great leaders know how to help people, they know how and when to assist their colleagues when the need arises. They know how to make the tools available, it's method of operation and also the right culture which enables everyone to give their maximum. Leading companies gives preference to their customers, they serve their customers better and then they are able to charge them better for the service they have rendered.

3 - *They maintain a high level of optimism rather than their pessimism*

People who are optimistic are usually enthusiastic and energetic. They positively affect every single thing that crossed their path, be it their boss, colleagues at work, customers, partners etc. Optimism is a character which allows you to try more, do more, take calculated risk, and ultimately, it makes you accomplish more. If you fail to be optimistic in everything you do, you will only move around and thinking about how things will go wrong rather than making a bold step and take an action.

4 - *They do not spend all their time planning alone*

Planning is a crucial part of operation but it becomes useless if it is not followed up by execution. Making plans is fundamental, it gives a sense of assurance to make a plan. This is how planning can be effective, once you have a well established plan, get going, execute your plans and see the results it brings, if the results is undesirable, you can make some adjustments during progress.

5 - *They never stop thinking*

A characteristics of a true leader is that, a true leader constantly project himself and his team, he delivers constantly, he inspires others and he doesn't succumb to pressure, and that means they think more often, they make instant decisions. They think about what is good for a company, what is good for the customers and equally good for his team members. His success depends on his ability to make crucial decisions long-term thinking and not only giving a solution that only last for a short term.

6 - *They dedicate voluntarily , they move before others*

One of the basic characteristics of high performing people is that they climb the ladder faster and higher than people who are reluctant to take on a new task. They volunteer for tasks which others are running away from, they make every effort to move away from their comfort zone even when they have their own problems. Great leaders don't wait to be given instructions, they use their initiative.

7 - *They evolve in full awareness*

An essential traits of high performing people is that, they understand themselves, they know the importance of not crossing the limits as much as they understand themselves, they also understand others and constantly get in touch with them. This understanding prevents you from blaming your failures on others. As it is believed, that "a person who does not take time to observe himself cannot be attentive to others." nor develops the qualities of patience required for exercising leadership.

8 - *They work their flexibility*

Change is the only thing that doesn't change, everything else changes at all time! From this belief, it is important to possess the ability to cope with changes that may happen according to the need of time. Those who are not flexible slow down (either consciously or unconsciously). Threat should therefore, be embraced rather than rejected, it should be seen as an opportunity, rather than a threat.

9 - *They share with others*

Knowledge and skills tends to grow rapidly if it is being shared with others. Keeping knowledge to yourself like a treasure may neither enrich you nor make you poor. Share your skills and knowledge with people, help them to grow, assist them towards the path of their development when you have the capacity.

Why some individuals, teams or groups have been able sustain that success over the long term?

Everyone dreams about being successful in life, but what does success mean to everyone? For some people, success means richness before anything else, for others, success means fame, power and prestige. For some, it means getting the desired job, forming a very good family etc. No matter what success means to you, you will surely want to achieve it.

Dreaming about success alone doesn't guarantee success, it is one thing to dream about success and working towards its achievements is another thing. Only few people are willing to work harder. In the world today, everything is nearly instantaneous, lots of people nowadays believe that success should be achieved on an instant.. This ideology is wrong.

In our environment, we know lots of people who are haste in achieving success, they look for a short term success, they are always after quick result. Moreover, this type of success does not guarantee anything in the future. Yes, you might have all what you want at the moment, even if it arises soon, it will even ends sooner. That's another reason why proactive people set their eyes on a long term success, there is a little sacrifice which very little people can actually.

Having a long term mission means to work on a long-term basis to strive hard to be closer to your goal day by day, to be focused on achieving your aim, no matter the wait, even when the results seems not too good, to keep on moving. Achieving long term success does not come easy, it takes a lot of physical effort and mental strength because sometimes you will work so hard but the result will not be coming immediate, you won't be seeing immediate results, this can prove difficult to accept at times. But with focus and good vision, you will know that everything will later come good.

Achieving a long term success can be realised after keep on working intelligently and diligently with clear objectives in mind; the time it takes to achieve success varies, it depends on factors such as social, economic and personal characteristics towards achieving success.

Why Are Some Miserable While Others are Consistently Happy On Their Journey?

Success itself is a challenge. Had it been it is not, you would have seen lots of people being successful, and for every person you see enjoying the fruits of success, there are many who are not even smelling the fragrance of success, there are many who are only examining it's roots. They are trying to understand what it actually means to be successful, they are perplexed and baffled by what seems to be a very strange, complex and elusive secret.

In every community, there are a large number of people who spend most of their lives struggling to make a living for themselves, there are also a smaller number of people who seems to have everything they wished for, everything seems to be in their path. Instead of earning a living for themselves, these small group of people are busy living in luxury while enjoying a fortune. Everything seems to be working well for them, while the larger groups are in a constant state of fear, being scared that life can be unfair and complicated.

Perhaps, "I am a good person, the man mutter to himself." why is it that my neighbour is happy and rich while I am always struggling with?" he asked himself." I have been a good husband, a good father and a good worker, then where am I wrong? Why is it that nothing seems to work for me? Life has not been fair to me. I am not lazy, I am willing to work harder than some of these people who seem to have everything going in their favour, I am smart, what else do I need to be successful? He muttered this statement to himself as he collapsed on the couch to watch television... But he doesn't know that you have to be more than a good worker and a good person.

Besides being a person who chases his dreams, you have to be a good planner, you have to be firm in tackling situations, you have to be willing to take up challenges and attack challenges if you really want to be successful. Don't let it sound as if you are having a different menu of activities, be assured that the process of moving from being a normal person to someone of high performance is not really difficult, but when you start having a negative attitude towards it, it then becomes difficult.

In reality, the process of anticipating all needed

efforts, changes and discipline is what weighs down the mind than in the real sense. I can promise you that the challenges you will encounter on your road to success are less difficult to deal with more than the struggles and disappointments that comes from being an average person. Facing challenges or overcoming them is a stimulating experience, proper feeding nourish the soul and the mind strengthens the mental muscles and this allows you to prepare better to take the next challenge.

Firstly, we have to commence the process of working harder on ourselves rather than on anything else. You have to gather more new knowledge, gather new skills and get new experiences, it is also crucial to discover new emotions. More often than not, it is what we feel that we know that makes a great difference in how our lives turn out to be. Our feelings about the possibilities we have and the options available to us determines how we have to intensify our effort.

Perhaps, you have knowledge and greater experience and perhaps most of the required skills needed to succeed, the missing item might be the strong feelings about what you want and what you intend to do. You might even be one of those who have become involved in the process of earning a living so much so that you have forgotten about the possibilities you have in designing your life.

After all, you have only one life to live. Use it judiciously, discover the things you need to do and try to outline those things you need to have.

Why are people consistently happy with success?

Success is a sense of accomplishment which rarely produces the lasting of happiness many expected. After achieving a set goal, new goals automatically tends to appear unexpectedly.

Man desire to achieve new things because they are quickly accustomed to those goals that have been attained already. The process of adapting to success is as inevitable as much as it is frustrating, it is also more powerful than you can conceive.

One of the greatest way to become accustomed to success is to pursue, what is called "a lasting achievements" pursuing an everlasting achievement is different to pursuing achievement that produces ephemeral happiness, after being enthusiastic initially, the pleasure accompanied by lasting achievements cannot be underestimated. Having a lasting achievement is so. Important that it draw a thin line to separate those who feel successful and happy due to their long term investment from those who plan for short term happiness.

Researchers from the Havard Business School made research on this phenomenon by making an interview with various professionals and evaluate them on the success they have achieved. The main objective of the research was to analyse what these exceptional professionals have done differently to achieve their rewarding and lasting career.

The outcome of the research shows that people who are both happy and successful for a long term do have a solid plan, they had a vision, a long term goal. They have structured their activities around four main needs.

Happiness: successful people do engage themselves in activities that would give them pleasure and satisfaction.

Achievements: they engage themselves in activities that gives tangible results.

Legacy: they engage themselves in activities in which they could they could transfer their knowledge and values to others.

Meaning: they carry out activities that do produce meaningful results.

When you engage in activities that includes the outlined four needs, a lasting personal fulfilment automatically comes into play, but when any of it is missing, a feeling will creep in, where you will start to feel like doing something differently.

It could be said that, these behaviors are the hallmark of happy and successful people because they address these four characters.

-They are passionate: For instance, Jane Goodall is a British primatologis and ethologist, widely known for her detailed and long term research on the chimpanzees of the Gombe stream National Park in Tanzania, she left her home in England and moved to Tanzania at the age of 26 to begin studying the behaviour of chimpanzees. This became her life work, she dedicated her time completely towards achieving this cause and this has also inspired many to follow suit. This is the character of successful people, they are happy to do what they like most, they have true passion for their job and have a complete dedication towards achieving their goals.

- They swim against the tide: To be truly a successful and happy person, you have to follow your passion and your values irrespective of what it may takes. That is one of the reasons that makes happy people and successful people different. You can imagine what the world would have lost if either Bill Gates or Richard Branson had played a safe game, or Stephen King had failed to spend every seconds left of his work as a teacher to write novels. To swim against the tide, you have to be willing to take up risks, avoid playing the safe games all the time.

- They finish what they have started: One of the most common traits of most successful and happy people is that, they bring their ideas into fruition. Great ideas have basically no meaning if they are not put into fruition. They feel satisfied in overcoming problems, complications, and in their day to day activities, they are open to new ideas. They know that a vision will be meaningless unless it is carried out and executed. That's how the vision comes alive.

- They are resistant: To have a long-term happiness and success, it is important not to be scared of making mistakes, not to be afraid of looking like an idiot and try again without hesitating. Recently, a study conducted at the college of William and Mary, various researchers interviewed more than 800 entrepreneurs, at the end of the research, they found that most successful people have two things in common; they find it difficult to imagine failure, they never nurture the thought of failure and they tend not to worry about what people will think about them. In other words, successful entrepreneurs do not waste any time or energy in dwelling on their failures, they do not dwell much on it as they see it as a small step and necessary factor in achieving their goals.

- Make your health a priority: according to the popular saying "health is wealth," there is a link between being healthy, happier and being successful. Health is essential as much as success, with time, I have come to realise that successful people does not joke with their health, they take up some habits such as good sleep to reduce stress, improve their level of concentration and get energised. They eat healthy foods and do lots of exercise, this helps them to have a refreshed mind and body. They feel strong and agile in carrying out other activities.

- They do not stop when they are faced with problems: When you focus your attention on an activity, your emotions will start connecting towards it. If the mind is attached towards a certain problem, negative emotions and mental strength will start creeping in, and this will hinder the performance. Conversely, when you focus your towards improving yourself and your situation can lead to a sense of personal effectiveness, this will lead to producing positive emotions and definitely, the performance will improve. Therefore, successful and happy people will not stop at problems because they know that they are more efficient when they focus on solutions.

- Celebrate the success of other people: when people feel unsafe, they doubt the importance of other people, because of this, they always try to be the centre of attention, and criticise people to prove their superiority. Meanwhile, people who have trust in their capabilities, on the other hand, do not care about their actions because their self admiration arises from the strength within themselves. Rather than focusing on the weakness, they do not feel insecure neither do they focus on the world outside. This will enable them to see things positively and see the wonderful things from other people. The result of this is that, they will be able to acknowledge the good things done by others.

- They think "out of the box." successful people do not think like everyone else because they don't want to be like everybody. While others are happy to live within their comfort zones, putting all their energy in reinforcing their beliefs, successful people challenge the status quo, they are open to explore new ideas.

- They keep an open mind: when you expose to a variety of people and you are always in agreement with anything they say without giving it second thought, that is not an attribute of the successful people. Happy and successful people acknowledge people, they understand the different point of view and always provide the opportunity for growth. It is necessary to practice empathy by putting yourself in other's shoe so as to understand the logic of other people's point of view. One of the ways of keeping an open mind is to keep one useful thing or an interesting thing from every conversation you get in touch.

- They do not let anyone set a limit to their joy: successful and happy people are such that, they do not allow their sense of satisfaction and pleasure come from comparing themselves to others, theb do not do this, because when they do this, they immediately cease to be the master of their own happiness. Successful people are such that, when they do something good, they do not allow the opinion and achievements of people to steal their joy away. Although, sometimes, it is not impossible not to react to others opinion about you, what you should not do is to compare yourself with others, but you can always tap from people's opinions. In that way you will not be much affected with people's views about you, your self-esteemed will not be undervalued. Irrespective of what people think or way about you at any point in time, one thing is certain, no one is as good or as bad as others say they are.

Happy and successful people tends to focus their attention on varieties of activities that addresses their desires, they do not focus on their immediate achievements only.

They understand that life is made up of the things that happens to you, either good or bad. They understand that sometimes there are some occurrence that you do not have total control of, and yet there are some that they could control since, sometimes, life present choice. For instance, you can decide between reading a book or not, doing a thing or the other. Life presents decisions sometimes.

According to the Stoic philosopher who later became Roman Emperor Marcus Aurelian (121-180), in his work, titled "Thoughts" said, "if you feel hurt by external things, it is not these things that bothers you, but your own judgement about them, and it is in your power to change that judgement right now." so, besides controlling these decisions, you can modify your perception of the things that happens to you.

Therefore, you should understand that life is all about your personal feelings of the things that happened to you, it is about the things you perceived and the way you termed them. You are subordinates to your decisions and attitudes towards things. Your attitude, decisions and feelings towards the things that happen to you will be the determinant in shaping your life, it determines your success in life. Your success is not measured based on your social or professional point of view, it is also measured based on your personal point of view.

In this chapter, I will be suggesting a list of attitudes that will serves as a guide towards achieving personal success and happiness, they are a key towards enjoying our brief existence in this world. I will also talk about the so-called "Emotional intelligence," its importance, its application and how to use it in solving general problems and some thoughts on what happiness entails. As a conclusion to this chapter, a set of rules practicable at the global level will be listed.

Attitude towards life: The Importance of Being Optimistic

From the fundamental rules of life, one of the basic objectives of every human being is to "build a meaningful life and enjoy the good things that comes with life." According to the great psychologist, Mihaly Csikszenymihalyl "one of the most important instruments in this search are offered by psychology." since time immemorial, many philosophers and psychologist have made observations on this problem. In recent times, the psychologist, Daniel Golem and has collected many of the works and has given them global recognition. In his book" Emotional intelligence" (1995), besides the success of sales, emotional intelligence has become an important tool in achieving success in life, either personal satisfaction, economic success or relationship success. This proposal has been widely accepted by industries.

Optimism: the importance of being optimistic cannot be underestimated, for instance, a test was carried out by a psychologist CR Snyder of the University of Kansas. In this research, it was observed and concluded that the academic performance of a student solely depends on the attitude of student more than his intellectual coefficient (Ci). Consequently, they observed that students with a more positive and optimistic attitude (which was evaluated based on special tests) tends to have good academic performance more than students having a good grade on the Sat (a test which correlates with intellectual coefficient). The School Aptitude Test (Sat) is carried out by American students who got admitted into the University, it has a similar intellectual aptitude test to the Selectivity Test (St) in Spain.

According to the research carried out by Sunderland, "students with a very high level of expectations set higher goals for themselves and they know what they must do in order to achieve those goals." He continued, "The only factor which could be said to be responsible for different academic performance of students who possesses the same intellectual aptitude happens to be the difference in their level of expectations."

Goleman adds that optimism and hope prevents falling into depression, despair and apathy when there is difficulty. In this situation, the pessimist do consider setback to be irreparable, they react to the situation as if it is the end of life, they do nothing to make things get better and, therefore, they do nothing to improve the situation. The pessimist should always have it in their minds that, this type of attitude is not something that you are born with rather, it is an attitude that was adopted, and it can be changed or dropped at any point in time. Everybody is responsible for their behavior and, although it might not be easy, you can eventually change your attitude. You must be willing to improve yourself.

Goleman then give its analysis, he said "it is the combination of reasonable talent and the ability to persevere in the face of failure and hardship that ultimately leads to success." Attitude is fundamental in what he termed "Emotional Intelligence" which he defines as the "ability to motivate oneself, to persevere in one's effort despite all frustrations, to control your impulses, defer gratifications, check and regulate your moods, avoid letting anxiety interferes with your natural faculty and being able to trust others and empathize with them." According to the Royal Spanish Academy, the empathy can be said to be the" Affective participation, usually emotional, of a subject." in general, it is understood to be the feelings of other people.

Defer gratifications, the attitude of knowing when and how to" defer gratification" has proved to be very important because it entails the ability to understand that in order to accomplish a certain goal, you have to learn to wait and work for its achievement. It is wrong to follow only immediate or short-term gratifications. Lots of researches have shown that those who have the ability to defer gratifications have the tendency of achieving greater success in life, while are more likely to end up in failure and dissatisfaction.

Goleman in his remarks, refers to education as something fundamental in the growth of emotional intelligence, he said "if we take the trouble to educate children, our children can learn to develop the basic emotional skills." furthermore, it is uncommon to locate schools that offers emotional control classes to their students, unfortunately, this is strange. As discussed earlier, no one doubt the positive effects of optimism and good humor on health and on our happiness. Later on, in the book, we will discuss more about happiness.

Problem Solving and Emotional Intelligence

American psychologists, Elias, Tobias, and Friedlander in the principles of "Emotional Intelligence" can be summarized in the following five points.

1. You should always be aware of your own feelings and the feelings of others.

2. Show empathy, understand and respect the view of others.

3. Face emotional, behavioral impulses and regulators positively.

4. Set positive goals for yourself and make plans to achieve them.

5. Use positive social skills whenever you are interacting.

The first point above can be said to be the most

important. It tells you about being aware of your feelings and the reason for that feelings. According to the author above, he remarks "most children who are having behavioral problems have these issues when they are narrating their feelings. They usually confuse being angry with being furious, being proud with being satisfied, being irritated with being sad and lots more." Although, the remarks target children and childhood behavior, yet, the message can be extrapolated at any age.

Methods were proposed by the authors to solve problems which are based on Emotional Intelligence. Logically, these methods are not without fault, otherwise, it makes you raise the problem in a serious and conscious way. Nevertheless, what matters most is that, it prepares you to approach the situation, finding a lasting solution and avoid falling into the thought that such solution is incomprehensible.

The method which is called (STOPP SPA) using the initials of the outlined 8 steps, this solution can be applied to all the problems of life. This method can also be seen as a method which can be used to achieve all kinds of life goals. The 8 steps of STOPP SPA will be discussed below along with different questions that will assist you in its application.

1. The Sentiments should stimulate you to act with

due reflection: controlling your feelings, general thoughts are important to really discover what exactly is the problem. These feelings should be checkmate so that it will be the first step in recognizing the existence of the problem rather than being the end-process of the problem, after detecting the emergence of problem, approach to its solution will be the next step.

The Question now arises: what are the feelings that you are experiencing? How do you feel? And how do you think others will feel as a consequence to your actions?

2. Admit your problem: when you are faced with a solution, the first problem towards solving it is to admit the problem, if there is a problem truly, then you should know that there is a solution that can be done to solve its negative effects. Ignoring the problem does not help you solve the problem, focusing on the negative consequences of the problem does not help you in achieving a resolution.

Questions: what really happened? What originated the problem? And then, what did you do?

3. Set your Goals, get a guide for yourself: it is important to set some objectives for yourself. Your objectives should be clearly defined and stated

explicitly, how you want your aim to be achieved. Your guide towards achieving your objectives is by setting a reasonable objective and having patience in achieving the set objectives. Don't be in haste, all objectives cannot be achieved immediately. Therefore, making a list of your goals is very important.

Questions: what are your goals? How will you achieve the goals? What will you like to happen?

4. Think about what you can do: find all the things you could do to achieve your goals. The more varieties of solutions you have, the better your available options. Because, just as the popular saying "life is complex, there is hardly a single answer to every given problem."

Question: what are the possible solutions you can provide? Are there other alternatives?

5. Preview the result: for every action, there is a consequence. At the end of every action you take, evaluate the result it brings, this will enable you to prepare better to execute the next line of action.

Questions: try to imagine what you would have done if you had your previous thought? What could have happened? What could those involved do?

6. Choose the best solution from the list.

Questions: Among the actions you have pre-planned, which will be the best to be firstly applied? What are the things you think will lead you towards achieving your desired goal?

7. How do you plan to proceed; do you anticipate the pitfalls? Do you improve your skills and persevere: once the actions to be done are determined, it becomes easy to deploy a good plan, if possible, you can test run the plan, then think about how you can solve the possible errors that may surface, and above all, do not give up when things do not go the way you want.

Questions: how will you carry out the action you have chosen? What will be your reaction if things does not go the way you planned it? What are the possible inconvenience that you may come across during the exercise?

8. What happens next, after you have known the result of your line of action? this is where the result of your plan is examined, success is not guaranteed, even after making possible preparations, but it is a ladder towards success. But, from failure, you should infer reasonable conclusions. Then you can start a new STOPP SPA.

STOPP SPA plan prevents you from, and shield you away from being soaked by the pressure of the situation, it prevents you from nervousness, anger, anxiety, fear, frustration, uncertainty etc. Another advantage is that, it forces you to stop, keep calm and have a deep thinking about the solution to a problem.

In one way or the other, we all know about the characteristics of some individuals around us, they can transform desperate situations into a serene one, the strength of their personality can make them overcome challenges easily. The quality that people admire in them is their ability to persevere, despite facing obstacles and setbacks. Justice is another attribute that people admire in these individuals, because justice is not only the most important attributes, it is needed to live a successful life.

The application of this method is not a process that could be done once and neglected, it is a continuous process. When you show interest and put it into practice, achieving a healthy lifestyle will not prove difficult, you will have a stable emotional state of mind, and that will definitely optimize your performance and lead you to greater personal and professional success.

To practice this, 5 practical rules are synthesized based on the idea of Csikszentmihayl:

The first thing you need to understand is that, you need to set an achievable goal, with time, you can then start setting more higher goals. Why? Because, the challenges of the goals you set will definitely force you to concentrate, and good level of concentration is required for enjoying life. Only an autotelic person will be able to derive meaning and establish its goals within himself, he will try to avoid motivation through anything beyond himself either external influences such as social requirements or biological factors.

For instance, one of the goals of student is to try and enjoy learning, for this, he has to start learning within a flexible and affordable environment, then progressively, he starts to grow to another level.

To enjoy life, you have to set clear goals for yourself, because, as quoted earlier "who knows what their desires and works with the purpose of achieving them are a person whose feelings, thoughts and actions are congruent with each other and, therefore, is a person who has achieved inner harmony."

When setting goals, it must be carefully choosing to avoid getting a contradicting goal, do that you can you can achieve your own aim in life following the lessons learnt from previous philosophers and writers such as the Frenchman Jean-Paul Sartre

(1905-1980). The Brazilian writer Paulo Coelho, in his novel "The Alchemist " (1988), calls it the "Personal Legend," the following quote was extracted, "All the people, at the beginning of their youth, know what their Personal Legend is. In that moment of life, everything is clear, everything is possible, and they are not afraid to dream and desire everything they would like to do in their lives. However, as time goes by, a mysterious force tries to convince them that it is impossible to make the Personal Legend. Love never prevents a man from following his Personal Legend. Unfortunately, only few follow the path that has been drawn-out, and that is the path of Personal Legend and happiness. They see the world as something threatening and, precisely because of that, the world becomes threatening."

Assessing and making evaluation of your progress is very important, this will indicate to you to either continue with your designed plans or remodify them. Life itself could be said to be the set of events you desire to happen to you, not just the things that happen to you

2. Perseverance, Against Failure

More often than not, the way you do something is a factor which can keep you focused and enjoying what you are doing, it might also get you bored or desperate. Therefore, it is necessary to persevere, despite facing many obstacles and get it clear that the pleasure you derive in doing something does not depend on what you do alone, it also depends on how you are doing it.

You should always concentrate on anything you are doing, whether it is studying, attending a class, washing clothes etc. Although, sometimes it can prove difficult to maintain maximum concentration in some activities you are engaged in, but it is crucial to be able to enjoy your activity through concentration. Without doubt, concentration is much better to do in some activities than in others. For example, the level of success you achieve while watching television is such that its concentration comes naturally due to captivating programs, contents, advertisements etc. Some other times, the image transmitted into others often divert your concentrations.

3. Setbacks are part of the Challenges

One character you should try to adopt is to transform your adversity into a challenge that can provide you with enjoyment. According to Csikszentmihalyi, he sees this character as a virtue that is "more useful, more necessary for survival and more likely to improve the quality of life". This is the reason why many physically challenged people accidentally mention their accident as a positive experience, because this presents them with the opportunity to face challenges, meanwhile, before they met their ordeal, the challenges were simple for their abilities. In addition, challenges can be encountered without the need for accidents, you have to persevere and find its positivity.

4. We are a Part of a World that DOES NOT Belong to Us

There are numerous number of essential qualities that ought to be practiced, qualities such as self-confidence devoid of selfishness and humility, this is because the majority of the people who enjoy these challenges do not exhaust much of their energies to dominate their environment, they always find a way of functioning within it with harmony.

This makes us to reach the conclusion that it is better not to seek your own interests exclusively but to be willing to be involved in the system whilst also thinking about the global system. For managers of big companies and politicians, having a global vision is very important because all their actions influence the society.

This could not be said to be a general way of

thinking, rather it is a philosophy of life, just as how there are cultures who have a great relationship with nature and their environment. Let's take for example, lots of American-Indians know how to respect their environment and take what is necessary for them and strictly theirs. During the arrival of the English, their indiscriminate hunting of bison and other species, felling of trees, appropriation of land and endangered their existence. This lead many of these tribes to go into extinct.

Therefore, the "global system" should generally include political, social, environmental, economic situations so that the consequences of human actions can be considered on a global scale.

5. An Alternative Solutions to Against Obstacles

Do not let failure or adversity to lead you to frustration. Because, frequently, people tend to focus their attention on obstacles that hinder their goals. The solution to this is that, you should be open-minded, this will enable you to discover alternative solutions that could prevent one from giving in and succumbing to the pressure of the obstacles. At the end, it is more common to later discover that those obstacles are not so great as it seems to be, therefore every problem should be given the relevant attention it deserves.

Taking the above into account, onwards, every problem you encounter, or each set back will afford you with the wonderful opportunity to make it into a challenge for alternative solutions to frustration and anger.

At work, it could be applied at work to have the required change in experience that the job could offer, although you might not be able to understand its effect at first, but it's effect in the long run could not be underestimated. Change the way you view work, view the challenges that comes with every job with a positive attitude, this will enable you to clearly focus on your goal and not to get distracted by the challenges you face. In this way, productivity at work can be ultimately improved.

Do not conclude that making problems relative could only lead to positive consequences. When you are facing problems, you must look for the best possible solution, that does not mean that you have to go through sufferings while the problem exists, because, in most cases, sufferings does not provide you with the best possible solution rather it prevents you from reaching a solution. Finally, in achieving sustainability in life, all these should be applied. By being respectful to the environment, the planet on a global stage, ourselves can feel better.

What Motivates People to Reach for Higher Levels of Success, and what practices help them improve the most?

Every human being has an energy reserve that are just waiting for him to invest on and utilized to achieve various success. This could be compared to spring at rest which is relaxed, but the fact is that, the springs of motivation differs from one individual to another. Everyone is not and cannot be motivated in the same way to be committed to a certain course, either motivation to do sports, to serve humanity or an organization.

As far as professional motivation is concerned, the same applies, some can be motivated and enthusiastic about a project or a particular activity to chase a certain cause e.g. to start their own business, whereas others will prefer having a dream job which makes them free and gives them certain life stability. No motivation can be said to be better than others, but one thing is for sure; if you choose a certain type of decision or career, you will have much more pleasure to chase the dream, you will have a kind of spring to get up in the morning; you will be MO-TI-VA-TED. And now, we will discuss about the types of motivation.

Becoming a specialist

For some people, specializing in a type of work or sector will fascinates them, they will desire to deepen their more and will dream to become an expert in their field. In computer science, mechanics, history or surgery, it does not matter. What serves as motivation to them is not necessarily about earning more money or becoming a leader at the company, rather sometimes, it is to be more known in their relative sector, or to receive rewards from other specialists.

Now, how will you know if you have a specialist vocation? This can be basically detected by asking yourself some of these questions, do you like to thoroughly study a question? Or you prefer to study several subjects on a whole? Being an "expert" is tantamount to thoroughly studying a particular subject, you are quite a perfectionist; in your studies you will often notice that you do not leave things undone except you get to its end. You should ask yourself these three questions: would I have the liberty to succeed if I have the hyper-competent in my specialty? Yes or No? - Do I dream of being competent in my field that everyone will come to ask me for advice? Yes or No?

- In a company, would you prefer to be responsible for specialists in your sector rather than being the boss? Yes or No? If your answer is "Yes," then you probably have the tendency of being a specialist.

What is the type of study that may be appropriate for you? Technological field will be suitable for you to pursue as much as you can, enroll yourself to school that specialize in your discipline. A university degree, masters or doctorate will make you become a specialist.

Types of available job opportunities include; teaching, research and development, a trainer, technical expertise or taking a position of responsibility in your field.

Becoming a leader

Do you want to take high responsibility, take a higher position and become the manager of the company? Many people, young or old do dream about this. But this motivation is only suitable to those who are talented and have qualities to perform this type of job. As a leader, you will assume greater responsibilities. Be ready to have good appreciation of the situation of the company and have greater spirit of controlling people. Being a team leader, he must be ready to lead by example, give instructions and motivate his team and bring out the best from all individuals in the team. To be successful and move the company forward, he must be ready to make difficult decisions, take risks and handle problems and conflicts.

After taking up the responsibility, it is then that many will realize that they are unsuitable for this type of task; they are usually unable to manage the stress or they start to show their incompetency in managing relationships among workers or team members. For example, they may later find out that they feel more comfortable with an expert job or on an independent mission. For someone with a real quality of manager on the contrary, he does not feel uneasy in taking delicate responsibility. He feels motivated by this type of challenge, he pays details to every aspect of his work, he likes to carry everybody along, he makes decisions. He has the feeling that he flourishes better if he is directing the helm of affairs, otherwise, he might feel sis-interested.

At a young age, how will you know if you are having qualities of management? Sometimes, many only discovered their talent in management only after starting their professional career: when they realize that engaging in too much specialized work does not fascinate them, they feel chained in their specialist field. Meanwhile, in their management and coordination functions, they feel comfortable. For quite young person, you can notice some temperaments of leaders, such as they like to lead amidst their friends, they take leadership role of every activity they engage in, that is why many recruiters do attach much importance to mentioning these characteristics on their CVs.

Three questions to ask yourself:

- Do I have the feeling that I will be successful only if I become a manager of a company or organization? Yes or No?

-Am I very happy when I am given the opportunity to manage a company while organizing the workers adequately? Yes or No?

- In a team, if a problem arises, do I easily take the bull by the horn and proposes solutions to others? Yes or No? If it is Yes, you may have the traits of a manager. The types of studies that may be suitable for your development may include general trade or engineering schools, studies that combines science, economics and humanities. Courses which may offer internship experience which enables you to work in a team and communicate well with people.

Having an autonomy and being independent

For some people, what they want, the kind of job they desire is a job that offers them with flexibility, a job that can make them organize themselves as they want, these people want a job that will make them feel free, give them autonomy and makes them work according to their own schedule. They will prefer to more autonomy but less responsibility. People with a motivation of this kind are characterized by self-confidence and a mind of independence, they find it difficult to accept instructions and constraints which can be ordered to them while working for an organization. These people are a kind of people who like to take initiatives. Have you found yourself so difficult to follow rules? Have you noticed that you do not like being controlled? This begs you these three questions.

Three questions to ask.

Ask yourself: - When you have a job, do you feel you always want to organize the team as much as you like? Yes or No?

-Would you rather resign your position rather than accept a position whereby you will not have your own autonomy, even if the job is paying you well. Yes or No?

-Do you think you are always confident when you are in the position of managing? Yes or No?

The type of job that is mostly suitable for a person

with this type of character includes; project manager, teacher, head of research department, independent consultant, Head of a unit in a country or region, Head of an SME, sales representative which is responsible for developing sales of a product.

Find a stable and secure position

For some people, it is necessary to find a stable job that offers them peace of mind, while living peacefully with their families, they want a job that is secured for their future while offering great benefits. They do desire positions in which the goals to be achieved are clearly stated, and in contrary, they do not feel comfortable in organizations whereby their objectives are not stated clearly.

This category of people feels attached to the company or the organizations that employs them, they are loyal to their employees, they do their job perfectly with lots of professional conscience. These types of people are neither "lazy" nor "homeboy." If afforded the opportunity, this type of people prefers to stay with the same company for ages and wait for a change in position or a promotion rather than try another company or organization to take up a more challenging and interesting position. Such a responsibility will enable him to gain seniority and gather lots of experience which are also valuable to his employers. Do you feel motivated in such a way?

To find out, ask yourself these three questions

- Do I pay more attention to my professional situation, stability and security, are they more important to me than autonomy and freedom? Yes or No?

- Will you like to work in an organization or institution where your whole career could be developed? Yes or No?

- Would you prefer to be in a position that ensures the security of your employment and that of your remuneration rather than a position which would make you assume more risk and responsibility?

Types of career and job opportunities include: all career of civil servant either in local authority or assuming a central administration role (those generally accessible by competition), education, taking up positions very large private or semi-public groups (e.g. Banking groups, La Poste, EDF, etc.)

Be an entrepreneur, create your own business

For some people, right from their youth, they

nurture their dreams of creating their own "business." They have the spirit of entrepreneur and are always ready to make sacrifices to achieve their aim, they take risks, accumulate debt, and spend all their free time to turn their idea into reality. Their objective is to set their energies and manage their business to make it successful; they will, therefore, be willing to earn more money, though it might not necessarily be for the comfort that it could bring for them, rather as a proof for their success. They do not find real interest in a permanent position of the employee in their company: for this set of people, this type of job is done to be a solution to accumulate capital and gain experience. Entrepreneur will not hesitate to take up the risk of resigning to make their own success. For business entrepreneurs, they often have their family, and other entrepreneurs around them. They have their "philosophy" integrated, it is very essential to forge ahead in success than to wait for others, then ask the questions? Do you have the spirit of an entrepreneur?

Ask yourself these three questions

when you were a student, do you prefer that your family becomes your source of income, do you squeeze out some capital from them to start your own business rather than relying on them to pay for your school fees and daily expenses? Yes or No?

Are you always watching out for business ideas that will enable you to start your own business, company or project? Yes or No?

Would you prefer to start your own business rather than becoming an executive in a company which is owned by someone else? Yes or No?

To devote yourself to a particular cause and serve others

Do you want to make the world a better place to live through your work? Then you need to solve problems, solve some environmental issues, help the poor and needy, fight against oppressions, fight against inequalities, defend the cause of life, find drugs to fight against diseases, engage in charities engage in different community services. If this is your goal, then it is important for you to engage in a job that allows you to live in service to humanity and dedication to your cause. Then, you should be ready to walk away from a job or company whose values and norms are in opposite to the values you want to defend. Conversely, you will feel comfortable growing and flourishing for a job that seems useful and helpful to your cause. The salary structure, its security will seem less important to you.

Three questions to ask yourself.

- Are you having the impression that, if you had contributed to the good of others, you will be more successful? Yes or No?

- Do you feel that it is more essential for you to use your talents to make the world more appealing rather than holding a position of responsibility in a company? Yes or No?

- Would you be ready to refuse a position which is contrary to your values? Yes or No? If your answer is yes, you will be suited to take up the following career: engaging in trades that relates directly to the service of others egg health professions, social workers, personal relationships (e.g. lawyer, psychologist), professions that enables you to maintain law and order (e.g. military, police), also, professions or trades that enables you to invest in service (e.g. manager, technician, logistician, finance manager etc.) what matters most should be, the choice of the company, its mission and its values.

Take up challenges, and win competitions

If you are the type that is fond of taking up "impossible missions," the one that likes to overcome obstacles and win difficult bets, then you should know that you are probably a "challenger," a fighter. If you know that get stimulated by getting entrusted to carry out delicate missions, or take up missions which are delicate, and others have massively failed about, example, saving a business from bankruptcy, doubling your customer portfolio, undo a social conflict, solving an arduous technical problem within a limited time etc. If you are the type who is excited and motivated to take up higher challenges, rather than being discouraged, if the challenge increases your energies and potentials, while on the other hand, you feel bored in a job where you have no challenges or where the challenges you are facing are not pushing you to your limits.

Then ask yourself these three questions:

- Do you like competitions (sports professional or intellectual) because it allows you to maximize your potentials? Yes or No?

- Do you feel scared to be bored to death in your workplace if you do not face numerous challenges? Yes or No?

Would you prefer working on difficult projects rather than becoming a manager? Yes or No?

Different types of opportunities which may be

suitable for you includes, taking up a career in sports, being a sales specialist, a high-level artist, or a strategy and management consultant.

According to Burchard, he said "It Turns Out That Just Six Deliberate Habits Gives You The Edge." anyone can put these habits into practice, when you do, extraordinary things begins to happen in your lives, careers and relationships.

Author of the best-selling books such as; Life's Golden Ticket, The Charge, The Millionaire Messenger and also the founder of various training programs such as Experts Academy, High Performance Academy, World's Greatest Training and Partnership seminar, Bredon Burchard is a renowned motivational and marketing coach, he markets the most requested and highest paid in the world. After he survived an accident, he decided that he needs to devote himself towards helping humanity. He devoted his life towards helping men, women, organizations and various businesses to express and discover their "office" inside their voice and help them to discover their potential towards positively impacting the world.

According to Brendon Burchard, he says "businessmen, high-level athletes, renowned authors and all other successful people all share some secrets which ultimately become the 6 key areas they have chosen deliberately, they have mastered these keys and exhibit them in their day to day life.

These 6 key areas are; psychology, physiology, passion, presence, productivity and persuasion. If you want to increase your level of performance, you have to increase your level of understanding and mastery of these six key areas.

Secret 1: Having Passion or Purpose

Your passion or your goal is what corroborate your general level of performance. When you have a good goal, your life becomes meaningful and the quality of your interaction with others towards achieving your goals is determined. Your goal leads you to be more engaged, more fulfilled and more alive.

A character of the successful people is that, they are always attracted to their goals, it serves as the basis for their lives. They are always mindful of their actions and why they are doing such things.

For you to boost your performance, ask yourself the following question every day

How Can I Serve Greatly?

Having an answer to the above question will really help you, it will assist you to get inspired. You will break out of your shell and think about what you will contribute to the world around you to make it a better place. When people see the energy in you in realizing your goals, when they see how focused you are, in reaching your goal, a relationship of trust will be created between you them, you will then have a very effective impact.

Secret 2: Presence

Make your presence be felt!

To be present, you need to be fully active, be physically and emotionally present at that point in time, you should avoid any form of distractions from both within yourself and your environment. Either you are with your colleagues at work, your partner or during a business negotiation, your success is dependent on your ability to be fully present, fully involved at that particular time.

Sometimes during discussion, your interlocutor may ask "Are you following me?" it could mean that you are physically present but not emotionally or psychological present. Therefore, in order to improve your performance, I'm the area of letting your presence felt, ask yourself these questions severally:

At what level could I be said to be present both physically and emotionally?

Ask yourself, on a scale of 1 to 10, what's your score in presence? You can then make the required adjustments irrespective of where you are.

If you feel lost or emotionally unbalanced, re-strategize, reload and activate your inner strength up to its maximum level of, let's say 10.

Before serving, speaking, selling, acting or even loving, try to get connected before showing your presence.

Secret 3: psychology

If there is an aspect that you need to master and understand, it is basically your psychology. Why does something of this or that happened? How do you think about it? How do the successful ones and millionaires think? How are they planned to reach the level of success they wish to attain?

In order to boost your performance level in the field of psychology, you need to ask yourself these questions severally:

Do I Live My Truth?

Before you answer this question, it is advisable to choose 3 words which describe the type of person you are (I.e. your personal identity) and also 3 words which defined your level of interaction with others (I.e. your social identity). Once you have been able to define yourself, question yourself if you have lived according to those 6 words.

Part of social and personal identity are commitments and enthusiasm respectively. Whenever you question yourself each day if you are living for truth, what it will imply is that you are wondering whether you are being optimistic, enthusiastic, fully engaged and investing in an ongoing interaction or relationship.

Therefore, you have to Live your truth, live according to your means and live according to your standard of life.

Secret 4: physiology

Psychologically, when you are tired, exhausted or used up, you will be mentally exhausted, and this may lead to having lots of difficulties in achieving your goals. The reason being that, the enthusiasm, motivation, courage and, above all, you will lack the strength to fulfill your obligations, cope with your duties at work, and difficulty in chasing your dreams.

Energy strength within is a prerequisite for having a high performance. High performance can be achieved when you have a constant level of energy which is not exhausted overtime. To be able to maintain the high-performance level for a long time, you must learn to maintain your body, refresh and re-energized when you feel exhausted.

For you to improve your level of performance in the field of physiology, the following questions should be asked by yourself several times daily:

Do I sleep well enough? Do I make sufficient amount of physical exercises so that I can have the energy I deserve?

In order to enable you to activate your body and keep it fresh, Bredon proposes some rules which a result of about 15 years of research work and experience in this field:

Every day, when you are at work, make sure you observe 1 or 2 breaks which is about 5-10 minutes during a work of about an hour.

Engage in 2 to 3 physical exercises (such as swimming, gym, jogging etc.) which last upto 45 minutes each 6 every week.

Increase your metabolism by taking about 4 to 6 meals every day.

Drink up to 7 liters of water daily

Sleep for about 8 hours daily to enable your body to restore your health.

Secret 5: Productivity

More often than not, a lot of people, when they get up from the bed early in the morning, the first thing they do is to jump on their computer or pick-up their phones to start checking mails. Accordingly, the first thing you are supposed to do is to prepare yourself to "attack" your day. Successful people understand this, when they wake up, they take few minutes to plan their day by asking themselves about the essential duties of the day.

To boost your level of productivity performance, the following questions should be asked by yourself several times daily, they are;

WHAT IS THE MISSION I HAVE TO ACCOMPLISH TODAY?

When you are able to define your mission, the next step is to define the task you are to undergo to achieve the mission.

Bredon Burchard offers the following advice to

plan your days better:

List the 3 projects you wish to accomplish.

Have a clear definition of the activities that needs to be accomplished so as to have progress in the outlined projects.

Have a clear definition of the 5 activities above, list the people you may need to contact to provide you with adequate information on each day to carry out the listed activities.

Define the 5 priorities of the day, listing it bases on a preference scale.

Once you have been able to define these 4 steps, here is the next step for you to undergo.

Turn on your computer, and connect to the Internet, if available,

Check your electronic mail.

Sort out the messages, you can sort by names, person or category of mails.

Take a review of the information that can make you move forward with your projects for the day.

Check for more information on the steps you needed to carry out to proceed.

Then, shut down your computer.

Dedicate little time to focus on you can accomplish your 5 priorities for the day.

If there is still much time, move on to how you can realize all or part of the 5 activities which you can engage in to define your project.

In 10-15hours check your inbox (not more than 2 consultations daily).

Secret 6: Persuasion

There is a secret which is common to those who build empires on the Internet, those who organize and mobilize an entire community, and those who have great influence on their children. The secrets enable them to be very effective and it grants them the ability to be able to influence a large number of people. These people all ask the following question:

DO I HAVE A RESOLUTE ENTHUSIASM?

In this world, the largest movement or organizations are being led by leaders who are bold and full of enthusiasm. These are unique leaders who are always ready to challenge and change the status quo. They are innovative, inspiring and optimistic to the extent that, none of their followers can remain inactive.

Therefore, if you are the type who always wants to influence others and get your message accepted, you need to be bold, enthusiastic, zealous, and passionate.

The more you try to improve yourself in the areas of the 6P, i.e. Passion, Presence, Physiology, Persuasion, Productivity and Psychology, the more you will improve your overall performance.

Habits That Can Help You Achieve Long-Term Success and Resonant Well-Being No Matter Your Career, Age, Strengths, or Personality

The directions of your life can be changed entirely by habits, some people have negative habits (e.g. gossiping) while others have positive attitudes such as "respect for others opinion." No matter who you are, what you are or where you come from, habits can either make you or destroy you. Check yourself, what are your habits and where are they heading you to?

If you want to be great, successful and achieve your goals and objectives, you must exhibit the right attitudes and habits that will keep you on track to success. There are various characteristics that you must gain and maintain, this will help you in discovering more opportunities and good things in life.

Some major characteristics of the successful ones are:

1. Study

Firstly, do not let a day go waste without you learning a new thing. Learning can come in different ways either through formal or informal. Make sure you study for at least three hours daily. Get books, watch educational videos, reading dictionaries, writing, seeking knowledge from coach etc.

Reading is the most important and essential among the listed modes of learning above. On a daily basis, try to assimilate as many ideas as possible, keep good books if you want to learn.

2. Set goals

You should make it a habit to always set a goal for yourself, write down what you want to achieve every blessed day, month, year and decade. This is a fascinating process because it forces you towards thinking big and learning to overcome smaller problems of life.

3. Planning

No matter the amount of goals you set, no matter how encouraging the numbers are or how specific you want it to be. If it is a long-term project, you need to set a strategy that is geared towards achieving your goals. Firstly, you need to break down the duration of achieving the goals into years, months, weeks and days. After having a breakdown of how your goals will be achieved, you should them devise a means that will make you achieve your goals.

4. Networking

You need to stay connected with people who can have positive impact on your life, stay in touch with people who can help you realize your goals, people of like minds. In this era, there are numerous ways of staying connected. You need to be a productive person, a producer, and not a consumer, to make effective contacts. You need an aggressive approach to networking and not a passive approach. You don't need to wait for calls or emails before getting across, make an effort yourself towards staying connected.

5. Keep a diary

Sometimes in life, you might come across vital ideas, innovations and important information, you need to tie it down by writing. This will help you make you keep such knowledge, ponder over it and ask questions about it, also you will be able to keep track of your stories, successes, failures, lessons, jokes and lots more.

6. Exercise

One of the secret to success is health. You have to keep your body in shape to enable you to function at your best. You need to be physically and mentally balanced, when your mind starts asking you questions, you must be ready to answer the questions. The best way to prepare yourself is by exercising your body and mind even in face of challenges or inconveniences. Once your body is at its best shape, you are on the verge of achieving your success.

Give yourself a good workout, imagine the stress and sweat that you will flush away, imagine the calories that will be burnt, that will be a great feeling, isn't it? Develop the habit of exercising your body at least 3 times a week, spending about an hour. Not only will you be healthy, it will also serve as the foundation for you to have a productive day.

7. Relax

Knowing when to relax, rest your mind and muscles is a powerful tool towards gaining inner and outer strength. When you feel stressed out, you start to lose concentration and control. You start to feel uneasy and uncomfortable, when you do not rest, you will lose those times which you are supposed to be productive, you will be working while feeling tired, you do the wrong thing and still waste your time.

You must find a healthy place, or things that makes you feel relaxed, for some people, they feel relaxed and calm when they are watching television, for some they feel relaxed when they are having a little walk, some, while listening to music or taking a nap. Find that thing that makes you feel relaxed. Even in the midst of a hectic day, find a little time to relax, this will assist you in handling your vicissitudes of life.

8. Affirm

The difference between a successful person and an unsuccessful person is their level of determination, what each says to himself. Every day, an average person talks himself about 12 thousand times a day. Say positive things to yourself, keep positive thoughts as the things you say to yourself might alter your life dramatically.

The other day, I heard a person saying, "I wish I was half successful as that person." many might find this to be a positive statement, why would you want to be half successful of another person while you can be more successful than such a person?

9. Practice your skills

Every human being has an innate gift which must be harnessed and exercise continuously. You need to work on improving your talents every day, if not you might not maximize your potentials or even, you might lose the talent. To become a master in something, you need to practice it so well, your willingness to be the best at what you do will lessen your level of competition as you will be high and heels above others.

10. Form a support system

Form a team of like minds, successful people have been doing this long ago, they have learned to organize a team. The advantage of this is that, you will form a successful relationship, these people will be feeding and supporting you with mental, emotional and spiritual support. People might be seeing you as a single entrepreneur, but the truth is that, you have a working team behind you.

Being Laborious

We all know the popular saying that "hard work pays," that does not mean that you are working for someone. It means you should dedicate your efforts to achieve your goals, your aims and your objectives. Looking down the history line, one could not point out a single person who has been successful without working hard to achieve his goals. Being laborious or industrious means that you are putting in much effort, working harder, studying harder or even passed through sufferings, than others. Being laborious makes you focus your attention and understand the importance of the attainable rewards of achieving a particular goal, and also fighting to achieve those goals.

Engaging in hard work, to begin with, you need to create a list of daily tasks, make a proper organization of your agenda and functions, and also engaging with people that can assist you. You should understand that you have to make sure that you are independent to achieve your goals in the long term.

Discipline and Consistency

An attribute which separates the leaders from the followers their level of discipline. For you to improve yourself and make changes to your life, you have to fulfil your duties even if you feel lazy to do so. Fulfilling your duties will enable you to maintain optimum performance and maintain excellent quality in carrying out services. Gaining consistency is an attribute which is linked to being patient, irrespective of the situation that may arise and the obstacles that you may face, in achieving your goals, you need to find some consistency.

Consistency and discipline are related. With good habits and characters while adhering to the task that brings you closer to your goals, it serves as a vehicle that takes you towards achieving your goals which in turn brings greater success.

Flexibility

The road to success is not smooth at all, problems are part of your journey towards achieving great success, it is part of every human being. Those who are flexible find it easy to achieve their goals and objectives. What you have to do is to learn from your mistakes, know how to approach such problems or similar ones should in case something related occurs to you. Learn how to get up when you fall down and seek knowledge to always improve. Even great men and successful people are known to have encounter one problem or the other in their journey.

Optimism

You should learn to be positive, stay positive and calm irrespective of the situation you are facing. It is necessary that you remain positive and trust yourself that you will achieve your goals and objectives, no matter what happens. If you are able to convince yourself that you will be sail the tide, then you are on the course of being successful.

Patience

Without doubt, it is not every goal that is achievable within a short term, some goals take time but do not let it overburden you that because your goal is big, it cannot be achieved. Let your goal be specific, measurable and achievable based on your current status, with this you can start working hard to move from achieving small goals to achieving bigger goals.

Practical High-performance habits that will make you successful

1. Measure your success in happiness instead of wealth

In this new era, there are key factors which motivates employees besides wealth, they give considerations to factors such as benefits, satisfaction and granting autonomy at work. They understand that, defining your success monetarily will only lead to you constantly pursuing an increment, rather, they measure their success in their achievement of true satisfaction. They make sure they define their vision, work towards it, and in the end judge their success based on how they are able to achieve it.

2. Challenge yourself and do difficult things

In this life, you cannot succeed without going through some phase which develops and prepare your growth towards preparing you to accept and overcome what is to come in the future. It is your success in overcoming these obstacles which allows you to learn and develop your skills, these achieved skills will then build up your attitude which will be a prerequisite towards your achievement in life. By facing challenges, problems and complicated tasks, you are definitely preparing yourself towards what life has to present in the future.

3. Listen to constructive criticism and the opinion of others

It is your responsibility to respond positively to constructive criticism, this will ultimately assist you in achieving your goals. Meanwhile, positive feedback tends to improve you and motivate you to succeed, negative feedback if not taken wisely can have negative consequences on your improvement. Comments and opinions of others offers you a platform which shows you the areas you need to improve, telling you about your weakness and sometimes "Threats" you can offer a redress to your weaknesses through personal training and development. This will in turn make you a better person.

4. Learn from failure

For some people, when they fail, it becomes hard for them to learn and move on from their failure, this happens because they dwell too much on their painful and disappointing result. Failure is considered to be the best teacher, although, it is easier to say than do. Yet, one still need to learn, move on and do not repeat the same mistakes. You need great capability to understand the lesson you have learnt from committing an error and apply the error in the search for success in the future journey. You can take a measure of making sure you do not make the same mistakes again by identifying where you got it wrong and dissecting the problems in detail.

5. Develop an early and constant routine to wake up

Studies have showed that enjoying at least eight hours of sleep each day leads to the production of high level of mental agility, having a consistent resting cycle is also important for the physical and mental stability of the body. The consequence is that, you will have a common rising period, you will be waking up at approximately the same time on a daily basis, this gives you mental calmness, it gives you the chance to develop a productive program and optimise your time. So, while others are still dozing off after waking up from sleep, you will be adopting a decisive action to empower your body and mind for the day ahead.

6. Choose a positive attitude

For some people, the fear of failing serve as a means of motivation, fear of failure will prevent you from achieving your success. Otherwise, it is better to adopt a positive and proactive attitude in all you do. When you take into account, various things that can have greater influence in your chances of success, it is important that you should take control of your point of view and use dogmatic approach as a way of identifying opportunities.

7. Make a commitment to achieve each day

Although, waking up every morning with a positive attitude should be encouraged, it does not mean anything if you are unable to make resonant commitment onto this cause every day. Following your goals and chasing your routine to success is crucial to your success; if you are not careful, the pressures of everyday will divert your focus. But, because it requires terrific unity and strength of character, it will eventually help you to succeed over a period of time.

8. Work harder than your competitors and those around you

You should know that it is important to understand that the success of every individual can be determined by the attitude of the people who are around you, although, you can control your efforts in achieving your goals. For example, when you are in competition with others for a certain goal, you should do all you could do, which is between your power without leaving anything unturned if you want to achieve great success. Your level of dedication is a determinant, once you make a commitment to work harder than those who are around you, that will give you a crucial advantage over others.

9. Make complacency your enemy

Complacency is one of the greatest obstacles to long-term success. Complacency starts to set in after a positive feedback or short-term objectives starts to set in, these achievements should be used as a spring to the achievement of success. You should still give your goals all attention needed just as you were dedicated to its cause before achieving the goal. Let's take for example, the former world best player, Lionel Messi, who despite being known as one of the best players in the world, he still keeps himself well motivated, he doesn't abandon his training and exercises, he still seeks to improve himself despite his achievement.

10. Do not fear anyone

Sometimes in life, on your way to success you will come across people who wish to achieve a particular goal which is similar to yours, those types of people may intimidate you, they may make the achievement of success a difficult one. You should not let these types of people to dominate you, do not feel inferior thereby subjecting yourself to undue pressure. Although, you have to respect people that compete with you, but to succeed in the same field as them, you have to dispel fear and believe in your talent.

11. Commit your goals on a paper

Penning down your ideas is very important, there is a potential success in having a to-do list, its application to your daily task or objectives will enable you to take steps which will enable you to monitor your progress. It serves as a progress reader, it shows you if you are achieving your goals or not, it also lets you keep to track of your progress with respect to the given time. Furthermore, having a long-term goal written down will not only serve as a reminder, it will also enable you to feel focused and motivated in the most difficult situations.

12. Surround yourself with positive and successful people

Having groups or friends is not a bad idea, but it is to your advantage if the type of people you keep are those who share a similar vision, goals and success as you. Let's take for instance, if you have a group of friends who always causes distraction to you while at work, you might be left with no options rather than follow their lifestyle or conform with your dreams and pursue your success. If you are the type who does not feel comfortable with elimination of irrelevant people from your life, ask yourself this question. Will someone who cares about my interest put my long-term happiness at risk by preventing me from achieving my goals?

13. Keep a fit and healthy body

A large number of research has been made to show a link between physical fitness and mental agility. According to the philosophy of Athletes Way, there are numerous number of lifestyle which can be adopted that will help you to create a balance between your physical improvements and your mental performance. What is obvious is that, having regular exercise is a key factor of having a good mental performance. Therefore, for you to grow the required resistance which will assist you in achieving your goals, a stable mental state is very important.

14. Invest only in the pursuit of your goals

As said earlier, wealth alone cannot be the most effective way of measuring success, rather, it can be used to support personal and professional development. Having understood this, spending some money on the development of business or career instead of spending money on material goods is a smart way of investing in the future. Knowing when to spend, how to spend and what to spend on is an important part of achieving success. Good financial knowledge will assist you in accomplishing your goals.

15. You must be prepared to make sacrifices

In your road to success, lots of sacrifices will be made since it is not easy to achieve goals. According to the "law of sacrifice," you cannot get something you want without being ready to give up something in return, therefore, you should be willing to make sacrifice, either by cutting out excess or cutting out unnecessary spending or even sacrificing your time in order to succeed in your career.

How to Get Ahead When You Are At Your Limit and Without Strength

The world itself is not an easy place to live in, this era, especially is not that easy. A lot of people lives in difficulty that prevents them from having an optimistic future. You should understand that no matter how worse your condition, even if you are in massive debt, do not surrender.

You have no excuse to surrender

One of the characteristics of the successful is their never say never attitude. Javier Echaleku has shown to the world that you can still get back to your feet when you fall down. He took a glorious step to stand up after losing almost all he has achieved. From having a company that generates several million euros a year to losing everything he had worked for, while even going down with debts. He narrates his story on his blog post in "I ruined myself by undertaking."

I am lucky not to have been in an extremely challenging situation, it is basically true that when you establish a company, you are always economically at the limits. Few begins their business with start-up financial funds which will enable them to compensate a lower income monthly or yearly. These are not just ordinary financial problems which you face, you run the risk of hurting yourself because your "initial dream" can turn to a nightmare if you neglect it.

You can beat yourself and achieve anything if you trust it

Everybody has moments where they get to a limit and in turn get to a breaking point. It doesn't matter whether you are an entrepreneur or a civil servant. When one gets to the limit, you find it hard to move ahead. For instance, a marathon runner might think he is mentally strong, but when he runs about 30km he noticed he is physically exhausted, meanwhile, he still has 15 kilometers more yet, he managed to finish the race because he knows he could do it. It is at this point that he realizes what he is capable of doing. If you are the type who does not surrender without giving it a fight with his last drop of blood, you will end up training your mind to be strong, this mental strength will propel your physical strength.

1. Do not blame anyone: Do not blame anyone for your misfortune, everything depends on you. If you truly want the situation of things to change, then stop blaming others for not carrying out their

duties well. Other people have found themselves in similar situations to you, yet they succeeded. Do not lose your energy in the process of justifying your failure rather invest in yourself and work towards achieving your goals.

2. Visualize success: Project your future success, then imagine the kind of feelings you will get from your success when it is finally achieved. Imagine how you will feel when you achieve the goal you have set for yourself. You should be clear about what you want to achieve and visualize making it a reality. As for the majority of the people, what they do is to take a step ahead of the other without being able to look beyond the third step. If you do not have any idea of how your destination will be, then there is no point in taking the risk. There should be a picture of how great the end will be, this will make you fight for it because you know that the end will be great. When you walk towards achieving your goal, see what awaits you at the end, and estimate its feelings if it really worth all the effort.

3. Divide the long way into small stages: When you feel difficulties in the magnitude of your challenge or problem, do not be scared off, divide it into

smaller parts, for Javier Echaleku, he broke his problems into pieces by paying the people he owed money one by one, with every one of them he pays, he has passed a stage, he will move to the next one. In the university for example, studies are not finalized at a go, it is divided into many smaller courses because if you should see the mountain of books that you will be reading, you may be scared and lose faith in studying, and you might end up without any degree.

4. Think about your family and friends: A marathon runner said, whenever I run out of strength in my marathon race, I do imagine that I will meet some relatives at the next kilometer, I do imagine that at kilometer 30,i will meet a childhood friend who I have not seen for long, at kilometer 31, my siblings are waiting for me, at kilometer 32, my parents who have been waiting to cheer me up. I continued in this way till I will reach the last line. Although they are not there physically, but I imagine having them there as if truly, they are there waiting for me. I will never want to disappoint them; therefore, I gather the energy from within to propel me further towards achieving my goals. So, I I'll continue chasing these feelings till I get to where my wife and my little girl are already waiting for me. When you seek to improve yourself, do not think about

yourself only, imagine the happiness that will be on your loved ones faces if you are able to achieve your goal. It is worth seeing that they are proud of you.

You should be inspired by the stories of the "finisher" to realize that truly, everything you propose in life is possible.

Thinking "Meditation": 7 Steps to Success

Nowadays, people are turning to the ancient practice of self-meditation for seeking peace of mind, clarity, and having a life full of purpose. While meditation is an easy routine for some people, it is not easy to practice. Cultivate the habit of self-meditation, it is crucial to your spiritual development which will assist you towards achieving your purpose in life, just as developing an entrepreneur mindset is the key to success in anyone's career.

There are seven steps to carry out a successful meditation program and star a life which is full of clarity and right goals. They are;

Align Your Practice with Your Lifestyle

Living an appropriate lifestyle is the basis of meditation, have a deep thinking about how you want to live, that you will be the basis for your meditation practice. For your meditation practice to have impact in you, you must also act in accordance. Just like in India, it is not compulsory to love in an Ashram (A place where a disciple of a community live around their master) and give up all great things, what is important is that you should be aware of what you are practicing, your actions towards your spiritual growth, mentally, emotionally and physically. Having an emotional intelligence, good diet and clear understanding of your perception will assist you in opening a clear avenue of information, ideas and energy to flow freely within you, during meditation.

When you live a life whereby you have no vision, no plan, where you only move from one thing to the other without surround by positive thoughts, words and actions, your meditation might also be in the same direction, it may also be like a shambolic whirlwind of sensations, feelings, images and thoughts. That's the reason why people find a serene atmosphere or environment for meditation, such as the beach, a cave, a high mountain etc. Having time for meditation can assist you so much, but you need to get the basics of the right way of living.

Stay Engaged and Show Your Will

According to the late Dr. David Simon, he said "commitment goes through a door of change, where once past, you will never intend to go back. If there is anything that can derail your practice of meditation, it is a lack of self-discipline. The spirit of meditation requires that you decide on your path and that you stay engaged every minute of every day. This does not mean that you have to meditate for all the hours of the day, and yet the only way to succeed at something is to do it on a regular basis".

When you are meditating while in a state of crisis, you might not get the actual results you want. The result of meditation is usually cumulative I.e. they add up as you engage in meditation day by day, bit by bit. For instance, if you have a successful training program, you will understand that the result of the program does not happen overnight, whereas, of your program was unsuccessful, maybe you did not attend the courses that you were supposed to take regularly, then you will say that the program did not yield the expected result. What you focus on becomes your center of attention. Commitment is the key.

Have the Goal And The Intention

When a person has a solid mindset of meditation, he approaches his practice with purpose. You might be having the intention of slowing yourself down a bit and take time for yourself each day, maybe your intention is to keep your emotions calm and your mind settled so that you can have a peaceful mind. Also, it might be that your intention is to connect a deep aspect of your life which you think is entrenched by sociological part of life and economical part - which may finally make you as a person.

Irrespective of what your intention of having a meditation is, you should try to approach it from a purposeful state of mind and mindfulness. For many people, at one point in life, they do search for their purpose, mission and goals in life. When you always keep focus on everything you do, you stay grinded in your "why," you will always have a reason for doing whatever you do.

Sit Down Calmly, Stay Calm

When you sit, you develop a stable state of mind that is good for your health, to be still and calm in doing nothing, while this may be an intriguing experience for many people who do not feel comfortable with just being witted, you can practice meditation through this medium, you can find it more helpful and relaxing to just be yourself at the moment, take a deep breath and meditate over the wonders of the world.

As you begin to develop yourself, you will train your mind and body in instilling some sense of calmness. You should plan to have some perception which agitate your physical body, which can lead to thoughts like "I am bored," "I do not want to do it anymore," "I might not be able to achieve it." This becomes your daily routine and your training ground. This situation grants you the opportunity to train your mind and body to connect to some phenomenon other than your permanent surroundings. You need to be patient with yourself whenever you are cultivating your ability to sit quietly for meditation. Also, know that whatever you do, you should not be haunted by the thought that you cannot get it right.

Practice Acceptance and Abandonment

Another important aspect of the process of cultivating the habit of meditation is to practice the concept of acceptance and rejection. It is normal for every human being to spend lots of energy while trying to control his daily results that others think about him, to fill his endless list of things while making sure that everything goes well in accordance to plan. It is not only exhausting, adversely, when things do not go in the expected direction, people tend to lose control of their emotional states, this then pushes them to work harder.

Understanding the concept of acceptance and abandonment, and its application in your daily life will help you check some of your attitudes and expectations. There are some advantages which you will experience during meditation, be it deep thoughts, emotional sensations, etc. These experiences will guide you not to be consumed by unnecessary feelings and judgements about yourself. When you allow yourself to submit to everything that comes your way, you are at the liberty of ignoring things that will later be useful for you.

Feel Your Emotions

Warning: when you are regularly meditating, you become open to your conscious and subconscious mind. In the unconscious mind, all correspondence values are stored, memories, beliefs and even emotions are stored here. It is common to experience different types of emotions during the process of meditation. This should not cause any fear, it is a natural progression.

Furthermore, whatever kind of emotion you may experience during your meditation, it is as a result of unconscious mind which is ready to bring all resolutions to the surface of your problems. At times, what you will need to do is to breathe through your feelings at the moment. During meditation, you can get a glimpse of how certain problems can be solved. What meditation brings into play is clarity, solution, insights to the problems you are facing.

Create Your Saadhana

The word Sadhana is a Sanskrit word meaning "spiritual journey to reach a goal." To create your saadhana, you need to pick a pen and a diary, think about the practices you will need to include in your daily routine which will assist your meditation, then write it down. After this, you have to act upon it by carrying out those routines daily. A saadhana will assist you in staying focused on your goal, intention and mission while reminding you of your commitment towards achieving such goals such as mental, emotional, spiritual and physical goals.

More importantly, you need to treat your saadhana as being sacred. It is yours only, you do not need to compare it with others, what works for you is all that matters the most. Most spiritual teachings offer that you need to nurture your practice by keeping your progress, program and practice to yourself. In today's life, people tend to compete and compare, but it is nice to keep something dearer to you closer to your heart and soul while cherishing it for years.

There are different paths that all lead to the same place, be it profession, phenomenon or life lessons. What matters at the end of the day is to find the one that best works for you. If you are new to meditation, you can begin by trying different methods of meditation. It is good and advisable to consider getting an instructor who can guide you through and whom you have a kind of mutual agreement. Take your time to familiarize yourself with the meditation spirit, and on the long run, carefully choose your style or path that will make you succeed.

Define real goals to organize well in your everyday life

Find yourself, find out your purpose, know what you want to achieve in your life so that will not be sidelined.

There are moments when it remains hard to keep up with the pace of your life, in such situations, you lose yourself in deep thoughts, you lose clear sight of your objectives and this obscurity affect your level of productivity. In the world of hares, being a turtle appears to be counterproductive while you fail to have time and resources to invest in it.

If you do not take some moments to think about what you want to achieve in life, you will lack the vision to start any foundation that will serve as the base of your enrichment in the long term, you may end up circumnavigating around the same circles in regret and frustrations.

In this chapter, you will be introduced to new strategies for setting priorities, setting goals and gaining clarity to stop dispersing.

What is productivity?

A definition of productivity

To some people, they think being productive is doing more and more. In reality, being productive involves being smart and managing your time, energy and attention. Having a balance of this aspect of your life is being productive.

For instance, let's take a Buddhist monk and a hyperactive Wall Street trader for example.

The hyperactive trader works at a frantic pace, having his intentions sometimes dispersed, he might not see neither the value or read meaning to his work.

The monk meanwhile, spends a lot of time in meditation each day, he thinks about meaningful things, but he works in an environment which prevents him from accomplishing so many things.

The ideal definition of productivity can be deducted from the meeting of the monk and the trader. True productivity lies in the ability to identify what is necessary, required and meaningful to the accomplishment of your goals.

To achieve this balanced condition, you need to pay much attention to time management, the concentration you give to things and the energy you dedicate towards its achievement. If any of these is missing, yob might not be fully productive.

- If you are short of time, you will do a bad job in a hurry.

- If you run out of energy, you will waste lots of time without doing much.

- If you miss a plan, you will feel disperses and disorganized because you will not know what to do.

Improve productivity by recognizing your personal values and motivations

"Whoever has a strong enough reason will come to knock down anyhow."

- Friedrich Nietzsche

This is the reason why, before you consider anything, you need to know your purpose and motivation. They should be clearly defined, these will enable you to create the best routine which will be geared towards pushing you towards the right direction of your goals.

The first step is to find out the reason why you want to be productive. What exactly do you want? What is meaningful and important to your life?

Take at least two hours to answer. Yes, I mean two good hours with yourself to find answers. We are talking about your life and what drives you on, this an important aspect of your life.

It is crucial to know what you are doing and why you are doing a particular thing. This will give you greater clarity and conviction in your actions to either work harder or change tactics.

For example, if you are the type who wish to spend more time with your loved ones (I.e. friends and family), probably because you are more motivated by promoting community values and personal connections. Therefore, you should try not to take advantage of a routine that keeps you far away from your social life.

If you skip this step, you may risk establishing bad habits that will work against you in the long run.

Another example is that you decide to go to bed early and get up early so that you will have more time to do activities that will contribute to your personal development. If you do it at a time when you do not have a busy schedule and you do not do it due to your strong aspirations, you might end up being unhappy.

Your answers should evolve during your life. That is why it is essential to update them to stay on course. Your answers will form the basis for developing a good routine and becoming more productive.

Think long term.

"There is no favorable wind for those who do not know where he is going." - Seneca

Once you know the reason why you want to be productive, then know that you instantly need to think on a long-term. Ask yourself, what are those things that you want to accomplish in your lifetime, in the foreseeable years, weeks or days?

Just imagine yourself at about 80 years of age, what is the story you want people to say about you? What are the projects you have achieved? What story will you tell your grandchildren?

When you start from the end, you will have the opportunity of outlining the contours of your operational boundary. In that way, you will start to know what you want and what you do not want, you then need to begin to make decisions and renunciations.

Macro level: this is the long-term goal or vision that helps you to see the picture of your decision as a whole and enable you to identify the goal in general terms.

Practical level: This is a short-term goal or vision, it gives you options to prioritize your immediate action and make you choose the most efficient task that you can begin with.

The micro level: is there to guide you and help you get the right direction in life; the practical level enables you to choose the right line of action.

Visualize the steps you are taking towards

achieving your goal to reach the pinnacle of your efficiency.

"Setting a vague goal is like going into a restaurant and saying," I'm hungry. I want something to eat. "Hunger continues to grip you until you order something specific. - Steve Pavlina

What is an objective? An objective is a formula that specifies and clarifies what you want. This is geared towards the actions you embark on to achieve your aim. When your goal is specific, you will be able to visualize what you want, this will make you feel hungrier to achieve it. The more specific your goal is, the more motivated you will be to take the necessary steps that will make achieve your goals.

When you set vague goals such as "I want to get rich" is not very good because it will not give your brain the chance to start using a kind of "mental stimulation" to have a glimpse of the desired result. You need to be specific, ask yourself these questions. When will you consider yourself to be rich? At 100,000 USD? A million dollars or two? Then, what type of richness are you talking about? Intellectual? Economic? Material? Social?

Clear goals usually record success in the "Everest Test." Here is an example: "I want to climb to the top of the mount Everest before my thirtieth birthday." This goal is very easy to simulate for your brain. Mount Everest is in Nepal, so you will have to organize a trip then, you will have to practice and perfect your climbing techniques, find a tourist guide and acquire equipment.

Once you are able to make your goal specific and make a conscious decision to achieve your goal, your brain will automatically every means to achieve the goal. Your goals will be useful if it is set in a concrete, positive, specific and immediate way.

Setting a positive goal refers to your motivation, your goal should be set such as it draws you closer to those things you want to achieve.

Setting an immediate goal refers to time, your goal should be such that you will always want to start now and not later.

Setting a concrete goal means that you will see the result in the real sense, the concrete goal will assist you in knowing when you will accomplish your goal, wanting to reach the top of Mount Everest is not concrete enough but reaching the summit of Mount Everest is concrete.

Setting a goal to be "specific" means that the goal should be defined, exactly as you want it to achieve it, when you want to achieve it and where. This will allow your brain to know in exact how you will achieve the goal.

You should also make sure that your goals are under the achievable zone, there are things that depends on you and there are not that is beyond your control.

Let's take for instance, you want to lose 10-15kg at a go, you might not be able to do this unless you amputate a leg. However, you might decide to pay attention to your diets and exercise daily.

Translating long-term goals for short-term action

To define your long-term goals better, you will need to break it down into short term action and steps. A good strategy that will help you to do this is that, you should divide each task and steps according to the time it will take you to complete each task.

Having an ambition (5 years or more). This are things you are looking forward to in the foreseeable future e.g. getting promoted, expanding your business.

Objectives (3 and 24 months). e.g. writing a book, getting ready to run a marathon on a competition, starting an online business etc.

Having Targets (3 months or less). The target could be to finish part of an important project, to reach that number of subscribers or to read certain number of books in a field etc.

Your objectives must be in conformity with your laid down principles. For each goal you set, identify the "what," "why" and "how." the right thing "what," is it for the right reasons "why" and in what way "how."

When you state these breakdown of your objectives, it will be easily translated, expressed and made actionable and concrete.

Assuming your goal is to maintain a healthy body, in this case, your "why" might be because you want to be a model, or because you want to feel good and be a good example for your children. The "How' might ask how are you going to achieve it? You may answer by changing your diet, eating habits and engaging in regular exercise.

At this point, the goal is not yet concrete because it lacks an achievable result and a specific deadline that will make you want to do more and estimate your success.

The moment you are able to set a period of time, then your goals become concrete. This could be, every afternoon, I will stop junks and eat fruits, every Saturday and Wednesday, I will exercise for 2 hours.

Priorities your tasks correctly

"The things that matter most should never be at the mercy of things that matter least. - Johann Wolfgang von Goethe

Once you have finished setting a concrete and long-term goals, the next line of action will be to organize and prioritize your tasks.

Know that not all tasks are equal, some task is more important than others. What should be your priority is that, how will you engage in all activities that will enable you to achieve the results that matters most to you and the result that will make you feel better?

Firstly, you can decide to start by identifying the three things that you wish to accomplish this month, then you allocate each week to what should be achieved in scale of preference. Finally, you set up your day towards the achievement of the most important task that should be achieved before the end of the day.

There are certain things you can do that will have a significant impact in your life, this represents your priority actions or "Most Important Tasks" (MIT).

To have a maximum productivity, you can create a watch list of about 2-3 actions according to their importance. At the beginning of each day, what will be your priority is how you will accomplish your MIT before the day runs out, unless you have an emergency task to achieve, all other tasks can be suspended since they are less important.

Once you have completed your MITs for the day, any other action you engage in for the day will only serve as a bonus since you have completed the actions is of most important towards achieving your goal.

Knowing your priorities will allow you to judge the importance and relevance in all your tasks, projects and obligations. Therefore, you will get accustomed to the fact that, when you engage in a task, it is because it is more important and essential to you.

The interest of the three tasks allows you:

To state your intentions clearly,

To make sure you focus on what is at the top of your priority list,

Not to be overworked,

You become less likely to postpone a task that seems to be more difficult in favor of a simpler one,

You will be able to gather the confidence that enables you to accomplish all the tasks you have defined.

Whenever you are faced with an intimidating task, keep calm, ask yourself, what is the first step I need to take?

Focus on splitting this first step into task according to priority, then repeat the above question. By breaking the task down into steps, you make it easy and less cumbersome, it allows you to progress.

Writing your to-do lost will assist you in making a daunting task easier to carry out, this will bring relief to your priorities by making it visible.

Three important things to remember when making your list

Plan and prioritize wisely by carefully identifying the most important task for your day and make sure you assign enough time to complete the task within the assigned duration.

Do not make the mistake of writing complex project at the top of the list. You can begin by listing the smaller, more manageable and easiest task to start with so that you won't get tired before starting.

Write them down based on how important they are. Lay down your plan on paper to enable its memorization and lessen the difficulties in your priorities by making it visible.

The matrix of Eisenhower

The Eisenhower matrix is used to prioritize your tasks.

This method of prioritizing tasks is said to have been inspired by Dwight Eisenhower, the 34th President of the United States of America, who would have once said: "What is important is rarely urgent and what is urgent rarely matters".

Breakdown of the Eisenhower matrix.

- Urgent and important tasks: are to be treated first, you have to do it yourself.

- Non-urgent but important tasks: are to be dealt with quickly, it can be designated to someone.

- Urgent tasks, but less important task: can wait, if not, it can also be delegated.

- Unnecessary tasks: should be deleted, do not waste your time in carrying it out.

You can designate everything others can do for you, while you focus on the tasks that have the most value and that only you can do.

Organize your schedule

"Every day, every moment, I have to decide what I'm going to do the next moment, and no one can make that decision for me. "

- Jose Ortega y Gasset

When you are able to setup your objectives and your priority task, what you need to do next is to start a schedule which will help you to measure your time and minimize the kind of energy and attention you designate on each task. You won't assign more energy than necessary. To start, you can determine the hours of the day where you have more energy to work most. At each hour of the day, you can assign a note of the state of your energy Let's say on a scale of 0 to 10.

The result of that is, you will be having an indication of the hours where you are at the peak of your productivity. Identifying the peak hours will allow you to assign those hours to the most difficult task and enable you to solve them more effectively.

Normally, the ideal working time weekly for maximum concentration and energy is between 35 to 40 hours. Anything beyond this amount of time will begin to affect your productivity negatively.

In 2012, journalist Sara Robinson compiled 150 years of research to show that when we work beyond 60 hours, any task we engage in will take twice as long as it takes to do the previous task. Therefore, in order to avoid going home at closing hours with the urge to do nothing other than ending up with the TV, computer or social media, we need to have a solid plan to assign the most difficult work at the peak of our productivity.

Every day, in the morning, create a schedule which is broken down into duration of at least one hour whereby you will carefully define your task, work and other activities such as the relaxation time, time to read, eat or sleep.

It is possible sometimes, you can have a change in schedule, if this happens, restructure your table. The basic idea behind the table of schedule is not to follow everything you have designed strictly, rather, the motive is to help you to cultivate how to spend your time judiciously.

Google Calendar can be recommended to schedule your sessions according to your goal (movie, learning, friends, family, siesta, sport, get organized), which is to be followed at suitable times.

To access these features: go to your smartphone, Google Calendar app then click on "+" and then "new goal".

Change Negative Thought Patterns

One of the concerns that you need to be wary of is having a negative thought. Your thoughts is another factor which can influence your daily life, your emotions and your behaviors. It is necessary to have full understanding of how to counteract negative thoughts in other to reduce its effect and amount of negative occurred. Interestingly, negative thoughts can be learnt to be reduced or eradicated by identifying the pattern of the thoughts, by altering your thinking deliberately, being optimistic in your thoughts and appropriately dealing with negative thoughts.

Identifying the pattern of your negative thoughts

You need to note out the list of the negative thoughts that crosses your mind. These thoughts are related to your feelings and behaviors directly. Therefore, the way you feel is influenced by your thoughts which in turn have great influence on your behavior. These three attributes (your thoughts, behaviors and feelings) all influences each other simultaneously. These three ideas are the basics to cognitive behavioral therapy (CBT). This is a type of medical treatment which is used specifically to treat patients with negative thought patterns. CBT is highly effective in reducing negative thought patterns. Numbering your negative thoughts will assist you in increasing your level of awareness of your thoughts and this will assist you in improving your ability to change your thoughts into positive alternatives.

Few examples of negative thoughts are "why is everything turning out so bad," "something bad will happen," "I know I will definitely fail," etc. If you are confused about what some of your thought patterns may be, you can as well ask your friends or families if they can assist you by telling you some thought patterns that you will tell them. They can tell them to give you honest verdict either positively or negatively.

Explore the causes of your negative thought patterns.

Understanding the source of your thought patterns will help you to identify the reason why such thought continues to generate. It is possible that past occurrence might be the reason for your irrational thinking. You should therefore, try to identify the situations that have been leading to each negative thought that crosses your mind. Let's take for example, if you begin to think that "I am a bad person" sit, identify the circumstances that might have contributed towards such thought. Some of the situations which might have occurred include things like "I promised my mother to buy her a gift and I did not," "I was punished for an offence I didn't commit," "my relationship ended up badly," "I was treated badly by the people I love most."

In some situations, it is very important to analyze the moments or incidents which led to this thought because through this investigation, you can start to see patterns of your thinking. What are the circumstances? Who and who are present? What happens at the time of the occasion? Where were you? etc. For instance, if sometimes, you think you are stupid, to investigate the patterns, start by identifying the areas where this thought tends to arise, where were you, and who was there with you. From this analysis, you may begin to notice the pattern of your negative thoughts. For example, may be the negative thoughts "I am stupid" was because you were late for work, either when you are alone or when you are at work.

Form your list in patterns.

Firstly, identifying the specific thought patterns before trying to change the negative thought is very important. Because, sometimes your automatic negative thoughts become your pattern of thought which is called your fundamental beliefs. These are also known as the useless thought habits which may sometimes grow a root in your mind. These thoughts do not reflect reality they are basically useless, they are thoughts that are not related to any other detail that comprises of people's events or life. Write down the patterns or habits which you tend to have. For instance, if your negative thoughts is "I am a fool," this pattern of critical thinking forms the basis of this thought. There are some thinking errors that are specific and common, such as:

The catastrophism: which is thinking that the worst will happen, like "Something bad is going to happen."

The overgeneralization: which is to reach a certain conclusion about your life pattern that is based on an isolated incident and thought "Whenever I make this mistake."

The reading of the mind sometimes consists of the weight that you know what others think. For example, "I know she does not love me."

The prediction of the future occurrence entails believing that you know what will happen, such as

"I am going to fail".

The critical thinking occurs when you have negative thoughts about yourself, such as "It's my fault, I'm so stupid." Having a thought in black and white is to think about something that can either be good or bad, it is without middle ground. An example of such negative thought is to think "she is the worst," "she is the best" and not to think "she might be difficult, yet, she is still a decent person."

Determine the consequences.

You should be able to know the reason why a thought is considered negative. This will assist you in having an idea of the reasons why it is required to change that particular thought. For instance, let's assume you discover that your negative thought is "I am not good enough, I can't succeed in it" negative thinking will automatically makes you feel isolated, having a low esteem or hurt yourself in one way or the other, these will be the direct negative consequences. Try to identify the negative results that has been the consequence of your negative thoughts in the past.

Next to your list of the automatic thoughts, is to simply list the negative results that may arise in harboring that thought, carry out this step for each thought pattern you have identified.

Keep a record of your thoughts.

You can make use of a spreadsheet to identify your negative thoughts on a daily, weekly or monthly basis.

Begin your analysis by identifying the ideas that sustain that thought and those that do not sustain the thought, use this analysis to identify the true thinking and the more useful thought. For instance, if you are able to identify the negative thoughts "I am not good enough," ideas that that will nullify these thoughts would be "I am valuable," "I am better off" etc.

You Need to Actively change your useless thinking habits

On your way towards achieving the aim of avoiding foul language, you need to stop using negative words. Letting some negative thoughts to develop and nurtured in your mind will certainly influence the way you respond to situations, this will produce nothing but a negative result. You should try, from your conscious mind to replace negative words with positive ones. Yes, sometimes you may go back to use those bad words unconsciously, it is true that everyone falls at times, but what will set you apart is to learn from experience, this will enable you to do better next time.

Make a list of the negative words you normally use, categories them into the black and white thinking errors. Then improve into a more balanced perspective, positive way of talking. Write these options down and start keeping notice when you use the positive or negative language during dialogue. Remember this technique every moment so that you will be able use a more balanced or intermediate language.

Search for the link between your emotions and your negative thoughts. Once you are able to identify your negative thinking from the positive thoughts and create another possible list of alternative options, you will need to pay much attention to your thoughts, change the negative thoughts and substitute with the positive ideas.

Make sure you focus more on monitoring your thoughts and have it in mind to substitute your thoughts immediately you realize that you are having a negative thought. Firstly, you can carry out this action by giving notice to the moment where you make the mistake of having a negative emotion, you can them think about the thought that have caused the resurgence of this moment. Take for example, if you feel depressed by yourself "Is this because I've been thinking that I'm not good enough?"

If your negative thinking is towards yourself, like "I'm not good," immediately, remind yourself of the alternative thought you have established and rehearsed over and over again, that "I'm good enough, I am worthy of love." you can also re-evaluate your story and include more details into your thoughts such as "When I was a little boy, I have failed at something I really wanted to do. Now that I am older, and I am aware that failure is experienced at one point in life or the other. You should say to yourself that, just because I once did not succeed, does not implies that I am not good enough at something I do. Yes, I have made some mistakes in the past, but now I understand that my failure in the first time in something I really want to do is not the end of success, I can try again and again, and practice until I reach my goals and dreams. "

If you keep on practicing, over time these positive thoughts will become instinctive. It will become part of you, you will be more skilled in that as time passes, but do not forget to give attention to your thoughts and do the required work to change them positively.

Choose realistic or positive explanations.

In life, everything can be considered to be either good or bad. For example, if someone gives you a bottle of wine, it may be because of your love towards wine (positively) or because you dislike it (negatively). One trick you should bear in mind is that, you need to choose a more realistic explanation and make sure you repeat it (aloud preferably). Then, you should consider the more realistic reasons why your positive explanation must be corrected.

Think more positively

Thinking positively could be achieved by recognizing the things that make you feel better, you can write a lot of these things. For example, if having pets around, a comfortable lifestyle, family etc. Are the things that makes you feel happy as you have noted the down, they will assist you in appreciating the number of positive things that are in your life, the reason is that, it will assist you in changing your focus towards appreciating what you have, instead of feeling bitter about what you do not have.

If you find yourself in a situation whereby things

are not going so well, instead on reflecting and wasting your energy on the negative side, focus on the list of things that are positive in your life, give attention towards the little things that sometimes means little to you, pay attention to the food you are able to eat, the shelter you have, your children etc. This will make you happy and grateful for the things you have.

You can also practice mindfulness to reduce the impact of negative thoughts, study have shown that carrying out mindfulness as a technique for reducing automatic thoughts is an effective means of check mating irregular thinking. Mindfulness assist in changing focus from negative to positive. People who are mindful of their thoughts tend to suffer less anxiety and depression. When you change your attention towards positive events, rumination which is an important skill for regulating emotions is prevented. Live in the present, not in the future and not in the past. Lots of people who are prone negative thoughts are people who spend a lot of time while deeply regretting some events that had happened in the past, or they worry themselves about what might happen in their thoughts of the present. Accept the fact that the past cannot be changed, but you have total control over your actions in the present which may in turn have impact on your future.

Engage in mindfulness exercise such as paying direct attention and focus on the things you do now, e.g. your eating habits, your daily exercises etc. Try as much as possible to be mindful of the present and enjoy everything you experience. Pay attention to your body, what you see and your sensations. Focus solely on the activities you engage in.

Treat each day as a new opportunity to reach your goal.

Every day, life gives you an excellent opportunity to set and achieve goals. The morning of a new day helps feel refresh, energized and focus your energy on positive things and how you can achieve your goal of the day.

Let assume you have already have a few goals you that you want to achieve in the next six months. Some examples of goals could be finishing school, applying for jobs, buying a car, making more friends or anything else you want to achieve. Set goals that are achievable and realistic. You can use a spreadsheet or create your own list.

Start each day by concentrating on what you are going to do to fulfill your goals.

Accept the change.

When you accept the fact that the only constant thing in life is change, this philosophy will assist you by preventing you from developing negative thoughts by thinking that your life is miserable, when truly it is not. Recognize that constant change is part of your life.

Although some situations in life might be difficult, situations such as losing your job or loved ones, yet some situations are unavoidable. Sometimes in life, things might not go the way you have planned them, try to see every situation as an avenue for growth or as a bitter experience which you can overcome.

Develop a personal mantra or positive affirmations that will assist you in accepting the change that might happen, such as "all is well," "everything will be fine." etc.

Deal with your long-term negative thoughts

Majority of the people do have negative thoughts varying from time to time, you can use the "Coping techniques" in overcoming this negative attitude. It is important to understand that, not only how to change the negative thoughts, but also how to deal with these thoughts are crucial. Let's take for example, if you lose a close friend, thought such as "oh! I really miss this person, I can't do this without him," etc these types of feelings are true, the person is dead, you can't change that based on reality. What you can do is to learn how to deal with this type of situations and thoughts.

Learn to differentiate between those types of thoughts, the one that needs to be accepted and dealt with and those that needs to be changed. If your thinking is categorized as negative based on the previously identified, e.g. Black and white thinking, catastrophism, critical thinking, prediction of the future, overgeneralization, and mind reading. If your type of thinking does not fit into any of these categories, this might not be a negative thinking habit. If you are to deal with a difficult situation e.g. the loss of your loved ones or having a bad medical condition, in these types of situations in which certain degree of negative thought are justified.

Another way to suppress negative thoughts is to change your attention or distract yourself with positive activities. This will assist you to avoid ruminating on negative thoughts. Another strategy that you can use in suppressing negative thoughts is to use coping strategies to deal with negative thinking and emotions such as forms of writing, art and expressions (e.g., dancing).

You can also find succor in nature, sunshine and fresh air, this can assist you in feeling better and change your perspective. Getting up, move around, reflect on nature can assist you in improving your mood and in producing positive thoughts.

If you are being spiritual or religious, pray or speak with the deity to whom you praise.

Accept the thought.

You should avoid trying to change your thoughts once you have identified it as being true. The idea of acceptance is a fundamental component of acceptance and commitment therapy (ACT), which involves replacing your relationships with your thoughts instead of focusing on changing them directly.

There is no denying the fact that negative thoughts do pop up in your mind from time to time, accept that this is true, and that your negative thought may have lesser influence. You should also know that not all thoughts are accurate, some are accurate while others are not. Sometimes you do not need to believe in all your thoughts as being fact. There are some ideas or thoughts that might occur to you which might not be consistent, you can decide to agree with it or not.

Focus on your general physical and mental health.

Your negative feelings might also be due to your physical and mental instability, feeling unwell physically or mentally can affect you psychological and this may in turn leads to an increase in the number of your negative thoughts. Having good physical and mental health creates an excellent opportunity for optimism. Therefore, it is important to take care of yourself most especially during difficult times.

Have a well-balanced diet composed of fruits, vegetables, proteins, and vitamins. Avoid drinking excess alcohol, ingesting prescription or non-prescription medications, or consuming other types of hard substances.

Exercise is another excellent way of increasing positive emotions and distracts you from negative thoughts. You can try new and creative ways to exercise, such as hiking, rock climbing, dancing, aerobics, martial arts, yoga etc.

Find a guide and a support.

Reading the experiences of others is a good way of seeing what is completely done to turn your bad thought patterns into good ones. Browse the Internet words like "positivity", "positive phrases", etc. There are many positive people who want to help others get rid of their negative thoughts.

Submit to a treatment.

If you are the type whose negative thoughts causes you to have extreme anxiety or causes you to engage in harmful behaviors, other treatments or therapy may be necessary. There are some signs that will help you to indicate that you need to see a professional. Example of thought includes; the thought of hurting yourself and others, having an irritating temperament or depression for more than few weeks, having difficulty in concentrating, having irregular sleeping patterns, having loss of energy and strength, having changes in your weight, loss of appetite, developing hatred to various activities you do enjoy previously, having a sense of uselessness or guilt, being restless and feeling irritating.

You might need to contact a psychologist, a professional counselor, a marriage or family therapist. Several treatments are used to specifically assist people in modifying their negative thoughts some of these treatments include: Acceptance and commitment therapy (Act), Cognitive - behavioral therapy (CBT) and behavioral dialectic therapy (TDC). The latter treatment is a form of therapy that helps patients in improving their tolerance for distress (giving them the ability to deal with negative thoughts and emotions), be effective in their relations and improve their skills of mindfulness.

Explore alternative ways which are related to medications. If you notice your negative thoughts are extreme (thoughts about hurting yourself or others) or give rise to a depressed mood or a recurrent form of anxiety, you may be suffering greatly from mental health problem. If this is the case, taking medications is usually an option to treat emotional symptoms and sometimes serious thought processes (such as delusional thoughts). Consult with a psychiatrist to give a thorough evaluation or discuss psychotropic remedies for you.

Having positive thought patterns can be contagious, so you should surround yourself with people that will make you feel happy and optimistic.

It is easy to transform negative thoughts to positive if you can start with something small, although the process of changing a bad thought into a good one can sometimes be complicated. For example, trying to repeat it that you like someone which, deep down inside you, you know you hate the person is an act of lying to yourself. This may simply not work. You should try to find a minute hint of the positive aspect and try to believe it before you can then move on to an aspect which is slightly higher and more positive. Basically, don't force yourself to think positively, keep in mind that you need to know what you dislike for you to know what you like while still accepting the fact that positive thoughts are part of the contrast in life. You can carefully select your thoughts, but do not be discouraged if you fail once. Instead, if you notice that the negative thought pattern pop-up once again, you should consider it to be another avenue to solve another piece of problem. Emotional problems have several levels and are sometimes complicated. The different levels can take years to be developed, and it encompasses many factors. Being patient while having it in mind that it takes a long process will help you stay calm when those thoughts pop-up once again. You need to be kind to yourself.

To Become A High Performer, You Must Seek Clarity, Generate Energy, Raise Necessity, Increase Productivity, Develop Influence, and Demonstrate Courage

There are various ways of increasing productivity, although at the beginning it may be easier said than done. Nevertheless, you can start by making small changes and stick to them until they become daily routine. Once you have created a daily routine, the other small changes that you add will lead to big results.

Improve your workflow

You should form your priorities while taking efficiency into account. Working effectively and efficiently is the key towards increasing productivity. If you have numerous tasks to carry out, prioritize it in a way that will enable you to work hard and efficiently. Although, for everybody, there is a different way of working, this technique will assist you significantly in boosting your productivity.

Generally, it is better to start with the tasks that you do not like. If you finish the task with fun at the beginning of the day, you will be tired when doing the less pleasant work and will be more likely to postpone it.

Avoid jumping from one task to the other. Whenever possible, invest all your energy to complete a particular task. When you have to divide your attention, you should spend at least one hour of time for each task. You can also try to include about five or ten-minute breaks between other projects to enable you to work effectively.

Take frequent and short breaks.

According to the popular saying "all work and no play makes Jack a dull boy." I'd you keep working without having break at intervals, you will get exhausted easily, your brain needs to rest at intervals to enable it stay focused and alert. Whenever you feel tired, take few minutes to relax and rest, take a brief walk, take a nap, drink a little water or take a coffee break.

Avoid taking too much rest that can distract you from your work. Especially, a "time on the screen" of the computer or television will probably lead you to losing a long session of the day.

If you have trouble in avoiding exhaustion, set an alarm to alert you every one or two hours to remind you of taking a break.

Schedule your time.

Create a realistic time table to work, you can make use of an electronic or physical calendar to turn your plans into visible reminder can serve as a means of motivation for you to work harder.

Include rest times, long and short breaks in your schedule.

Try to treat your schedule carefully, take it gradually, don't jump into it, especially when you just start. At the end of the scheduled work day, take few minutes to write a scheduled plan for the next day.

Motivate yourself with the rewards.

When you set either a short or long-term goal for yourself, set a reward for yourself that will be earned at the end of each achievement. For smaller goals such as finishing the laundry service on a Saturday, you can reward yourself with an ice cream or use half an hour to engage in an activity you so much love. For bigger goals such as graduating with a certain grade, take a vacation or an adventure.

Avoid committing to too many projects.

Give your goal all the required attention and effort while avoiding unnecessary extensions. Having a quick and professional results is more effective and more appreciated than having some extra weeks of extension. Have a firm desire of going beyond what is required for projects that are very important.

Create an efficient workspace

At your workplace, make sure your workspace is well organized, if you are the type who always have a desk full of papers, make sure you take some minutes to arrange everything in order. This is an activity that brings orderliness to your work and can increase your daily efficiency, once you have finished with the proper arrangements, the below tips will guide you:

- Materials or instruments which you use frequently must be in a visible and accessible area.

- If you are the type who often forget where things are kept, tag the drawers and cabinets.

- Return everything to its correct place after using it.

Find a private space.

If your workplace is located in a public area with frequent modes of interruptions, create a more private space to work, if this could not be done, try to work in an environment surrounded by positive and productive people. Avoid spending time in the company of people who are not on the same page with you or those who are source of distractions to you.

Even if the majority of your work is on a desktop, you can think of some tasks that you can print and finish by hand in a quieter place.

Minimize electronic distractions.

This can prove to be difficult, especially when most of the work you do is on a computer or telephone. You can minimize distractions by turning off all electronic devices that does not correspond to your activity at the moment and take some additional measures to avoid distractions. Such as:

- Blocking all the websites that distract you.

- Closing all non-essential websites.

- If you need to have your phone turned on to receive calls, turn off the Wi-Fi to slow down the speed of the Internet.

- If you tend to be distracted by video games or other software applications, create a separate work account on your computer.

Switch from printed documents to electronic ones.

Sometimes you are the type of person who is usually confused every time with finding the right paper or document, you can always make use of the electronic documents. Most organizations and banks nowadays allows you to sign up to receive your bills online. If you handle a large work documents, consider the idea of having electronic copies.

As a last option, scan the documents yourself and save it to create PDF files, this will allow you to have a database that performs easy search operation.

Create a reliable file system

Irrespective of whether or not you handle a physical filing cabinet or an electronic file, you need to create a filing system that gives you intuitive access. Make sure you organize all the electronic files into a well named folder for easy identification.

Starting the name of each file a folder name or with the date in YYYYMMDD format is an easy and universal system for easy file retrieval. As an alternative, you can start with the name of the client or the name of the project.

Improve your physical and mental alertness

Have a regular sleeping routine. This is a very important tool to stay alert and productive. Even on those days which you do not go to work or holidays, stick to your regular sleeping schedule as much as you can to get up and go to bed.

Have a healthy diet

Healthy diet should include a large number of vitamins, healthy carbohydrates, proteins, healthy fats and fiber. Eating foods that are rich in carbohydrates, including fast foods, can foods, processed foods and desserts, causes a drop-in sugar content of the blood, this may make it difficult to get through the day without getting exhausted.

Keep some healthy snacks close to your work space, especially if you are the type who is found of postponing things when preparing your sandwiches.

Be careful with caffeine

Taking coffee or other energy drinks will truly boost your energy level, but it is only for a short time, at the end, there will be a downturn. Do not make it a habit of taking this drinks, except for some moderate amount and on special occasions. Daily consumption of caffeine drinks will only make you dependent on the drink, you will only become addicted to the drink, it will force you to continue having the drink till it reaches some level of discomfort whereby you won't be able to carry out any action without the substance. If this happens to you, consider quitting caffeine to have a more effective workday.

Exercise

Exercise for at least 30 minutes daily to maintain energy and health. Just waking up to some squats and push-ups will make you feel energetic and stay more alert throughout the day.

Allow yourself to relax

Once you are through with the day's work, do take some time to relax. Do anything that makes you feel "relaxed and recharged." it might be a hangout with friends, a quiet night at home or a nice time at the cinema. You should also make sure you take some days off, from time to time to avoid running out, let someone take care of the children or take a day off from work.

Pay attention to your emotions

Running away from relationship problems or family problems is not the best solution, it won't make them go away. Taking your emotions to work will prevent you from giving 100% concentration. The best thing to do is to try to address these problems. Meanwhile, try to free up your mind as much as possible, meditate, exercise or talk to a confidant or trusted friend.

Nine Talents of People Who Do Better Than Others

Have you ever asked yourself these question, why have you been successful in achieving some of your goals while you have failed in others? If you are not so sure of the answer, we'll, you are far from being alone in this case. It is not funny that even the highly accomplished people, the brilliant people etc. are unable to give explanation to the reason why they succeed or fail in some respects. Intuitively, just by predisposition, people are blessed with some talents which others do not have. In fact, lots of research into success have suggested that successful people achieve their goals not because of what they are, but more than often, it was because of what they do. The nine hidden talents are:

1. Be specific

When you set a goal, try to make sure your goal is as specific as possible, take for example "Losing 10 pounds" is a more specific goal than "Losing weight" because it gives you a clear definition of what your success will look like. Having knowledge of what you want to achieve will keep you motivated until you get there. Also, think in detail about the actions you need to engage in to reach your goal. Being contented with the promise you made to yourself that you will "eat less" or that you will "sleep more" is a goal that is not clearly defined. Be clear and precise while setting up your goal; "During the week, I will go to bed at 10 pm", that leaves no room for doubt about what you have decided to do and how to control whether you were able to do it or not.

2. Find the time to focus on achieving your goals

It is not surprising that sometimes people regularly miss opportunities to pursue a specific goal because they have lots of agenda and numerous number of goals which they want to achieve at the same time. Having a specific goal and time to focus on achieving a goal at a time is highly essential.

For you to reach your goals, you have to seize every opportunity that comes your way before it slips through your fingers. To seize an opportunity, you have to have prior knowledge of when and where you will devote them. While keeping in mind that you have to be "Specific" for example, during the week days, I will dedicate an hour of my time for exercises. Research has shown that this type of plan will help you to seize and identify an opportunity anytime it presents itself, studies also show that it increases your chances of success by more than 100%.

3. Know exactly how far you need to go

In achieving your goals, you will need a regular monitoring of the progress of your project. You can monitor how far you have gone in achieving your goal or let others monitor your progress, if you fail to appreciate the quality of your actions, you will not be able to adjust your strategies and behavior. Constantly check the progress of your work; every day, every week or month, depending on your goal.

4. Be a realistic optimist

Whenever you set a goal, adopt all measures that will enable you to reach such goal by adopting a positive state of mind. You also need to believe in your ability to succeed, this is essential to support your motivation. Whenever you are carrying out an operation which is geared towards achieving your goal, do not underestimate your chances of achieving your goal. To achieve your goal, time, effort, planning and perseverance is important. Studies have shown that, when you think that some things will come to you easily without making adequate effort leads to poor preparation which will increase your chances of failure than your chances of success.

5. Focus on becoming better rather than being good

Your belief in yourself is very crucial, believing that you have the potential to achieve your goal and you believing that you can gain that potential is equally necessary. Some people think that their intelligence, physical ability or personality is fixed in whatever they do, they do not want to increase their pace. As a result, they focus on the goal that they want to achieve rather than acquiring and developing new skills that will enable them to achieve their goal.

Studies have shown that "everyone's potential is not static" it is very flexible and can be improved towards any length. Accepting the fact that you can improve will definitely allow you to make better choices and allow you to reach your optimum level of success. People who have a goal of becoming better rather than good, embrace problems and difficulties without being outweighed, they believe in the happiness of reaching their goals.

6. Have some guts

Your desire and willingness to commit yourself to long term goals and to persist in the face of tribulations is known as "Guts." studies have shown that people who have guts are the ones who, during their lifetime, get the best grades, achieve the most difficult things, get the most education etc. The "notch" factor has infarct predicts the cadets at West Point who will emerge successful after the completion of their difficult first year in the university. In fact, this "Notch" will also predict which candidate will record success at the National Spelling Bee competition (This competition in the United States is an annual contest in which young children will be told to spell words chosen by panelists, whereby the competitor who gets it wrong will be eliminated until there is only one winner). Lacking guts will make you to believe that you do not have the innate ability of the people who succeeds. If that thought do cross you mind... You are wrong! As I have explained above, putting in effort, perseverance, good plan, and good strategy will lead you to success. These attributes will help you get better in visualizing your objectives, it will also assist you in gaining guts effort, planning, perseverance and having good strategies will ultimately lead you to success. While you adopt these characteristics, you won't only have a better glimpse of your success, you will also have the guts to achieve your goals.

7. Muscle your will

Muscle of self-control, just like the muscle in your body get weakens when not in use or stressed, it weakens overtime, but when you exercise and train it regularly, it becomes better and stronger to enable you to achieve your goal.

To develop you " muscle of will" you have to choose an activity that requires you to do some things that you will rather not do e.g. trying to learn a new skill, stop high fat junks, sit a hundred times a day... etc.

When you are about to submit to your inability, don't give up, restructure strategize, start by attending to one task at a time and anticipate how happy you will be when you succeed in handling the problem. For instance, if you love to take fast food, then you will inculcate the habit of fresh fruits as a supplement. At first, this may seem to be a daunting task, but on the long run, it becomes easier. As your strength in coping improves, you can then set new challenges and intensify your self-control training.

8. Do not attempt the spell

Regardless of how strong you are, both mentally and physically, you should always respect the fact that your strength is limited and, if you ask too much of it, you might get to a breaking point. Try as much as possible to avoid tackling two challenges at once e.g. quitting smoking and dieting simultaneously. Lots of people overestimate their ability to withstand temptation, do, instead of trying to avoid temptations as much as possible, they put themselves in situations that abound temptation. Successful people do not make it harder for themselves to reach their goals.

9. Focus on what you will do, not what you will not do

Do you want to be physically fit, then you need a good diet and a good fitness program. What you should do is to plan how you will substitute your bad habits with good ones, rather than being preoccupied with your bad habits. Dwell more on the involuntary rejection of painful thoughts. Studies have shown that while trying to dismiss a thought, you might end up making it more meaningful to the mind. Same as behavior, when you are striving not to submit to a bad habit, if you are not careful, you might end up strengthening the habit, rather than breaking free of the habit.

If you are planning to eradicate some of your behaviors, ask yourself these simple questions, "what behavior will I replace it with?" example, if your aim is to control anger, you could devise a plan that "anytime I feel angry, If I am standing, I will sit down, if I am sitting, I will lay down, if I don't feel calm, I will take some water to calm myself down." changing position to suppress anger and engaging in actions to substitute the bad habits, overtime your bad habit will fade away, it will eventually disappear.

I hope that after reading "The 9 things that successful people do differently than others," you have gotten some ideas about what you have been doing well or doing wrong. More importantly, I hope you are now able to identify the habits that have been derailing you and be able to fix them. And do remember this: you do not have to become a different person to become a successful person.

www.ingramcontent.com/pod-product-compliance
Lightning Source LLC
Chambersburg PA
CBHW070905080526
44589CB00013B/1182